Computer Networking
First Steps

Table of Contents

Introduction

Congratulations on downloading your copy of *Computer Networking First Step.* It is a source of delight to me that you chose his book as you set out on a journey to learning more about computer networking. Computer networking is an important part of our lives in the workplace, at school, and even at home, and that is why many seek to understand how computers connect with each other.

As you continue to read, you will discover that networking is versatile and that different people may understand it differently depending on the part of the network that they are handling. However, you will understand that networks are what connects computers at the basic LAN level and even further as the networks extends over larger geographical areas.

While you may have never thought of networking in detail, this book will introduce you to the basics of networking, the different types of networks available, the types of network topologies that you will encounter, the concept of server virtualization, and details of how to handle network breaches. The book also offers an explanation of network protocols, design, and infrastructure—information that will help you understand how computers interact with each other.

There are indeed a variety of books that have been written about computer networking, and it is a privilege that you should choose this book to help you advance in the field, even in the slightest. Thank you for choosing this title. As a token of appreciation, every effort was made to ensure that this book carries only the most up-to-date information that will be useful for you, whether you are a starter at networking or are already established in the field.

Chapter 1: Basics of a Network

This chapter outlines the basics of networking. As a starter, you probably have no idea what the term network means, or you may just have a slight idea. Do not worry because that is the purpose of this book. In the next sections, you will understand the definition of a network and the different types of networks, depending on whether you are cabling, working on networking devices, or servers. You shall also understand in detail the servers, clients, big and small networks, topology, and network administration.

Definition of a Network and Why It Exists

There are networks almost everywhere in the world. Look at your body; for instance, there are various networks of tissues, organs, and cells that allow your body to work efficiently. Even in plants, it is easy to see a network of leaves and branches that lead to the stems and, finally, roots. The concept of networks, however, has defied the natural world and has permeated virtually into every aspect of our lives. There are human networks that enable us to connect with one another at home, at school, and even at work. In this chapter, we focus on computer networks and how the components of the network communicate with each other

When it comes to the concept of computer networks and networking, it is important to understand that different people understand it differently. Going forward, you may realize that you come to your own conclusions and understanding of this concept. This notion simply means that even as you begin to understand networks, you should not really judge the next person's perception of the same. Also, the fact that you will understand networking differently shows you that this is a technical field and there are many interconnections involved. Therefore, finding an efficient order in which to present the world of networking may be difficult. The approach in this book, however, is friendly and takes a path that you are likely to understand without a lot of stress. Dive in for some more.

A network, essentially, is an amalgamation of different components, including hardware, software, and cabling that allows communication between multiple computing devices.

The essentials that will be presented in this chapter are:

- LANs- Local area networks

- IP-Internet protocols

- TCP- Transport and connections protocol

The three essentials mentioned above are also known as layers. LANs are the link layer; the internet is the work layer, and TCP is the transport layer. There is another type of layer, the application layer, which constitutes the software that you use. Together, they form the four-layer model that is known in networking. In this context, you can view a layer as a library, and each layer communicates with the layers that directly border it. The application layer will, therefore, communicate a set of data to the transport and connections protocol library, which will, in turn, communicate with the internet protocol library, which will further communicate with the LAN to ensure the delivery of the message. As such, the application does not have direct interaction with the other parts of the network, such as the IP and LAN.

The LAN layer is the one responsible for the delivery of data pockets through LAN-layer supplied addresses. LAN is divided into the logical and physical component. The logical component comprises the abstract LAN layer that is digital, while the physical layer is often the optical or electrical signaling mechanism involved. The physical layer of the LAN concerns the designers of physical hardware. The five-layer model, as represented below, comes as a result of the LAN'S physical/logical division.

| Application |
| Transport |
| IP |
| Logical LAN |
| Physical LAN |

The explanation that follows will follow a logical model that will see the reader oscillating between concepts to fully understand how networks operate.

What Is a Client/Server Network?

This is a network in which a centralized and often more powerful machine or computer, also referred to as the server, works as a hub that supports less powerful workstations or computers, also referred to as clients. The clients are connected to the server and run programs and access data that are already existent or stored on the server. The server is, therefore, designed and dedicated to the running of services that serve the needs of other computers within the network. The server could be a database, file, print, home media, or web server, depending on the running service. The client, on the other hand, is not necessarily a computer but can be a computer software or hardware that accesses the services of the servers. Often, servers are located on separate physical computers, but sometimes, they can be connected within the same system. The client, typically, does not share its resources but requests the service function and content of a server. Therefore, clients will initiate communication with the server that will usually be waiting for incoming requests.

When looking at the roles of servers and clients, you will realize that servers are classified based on the role of the play and services provided. For instance, the file server serves computer files, while web server provides services for web pages. The resources shared may vary from data, processors, programs, and storage devices, and this sharing of server resources constitutes a service.

The image below shows a set-up of the network client relationship:

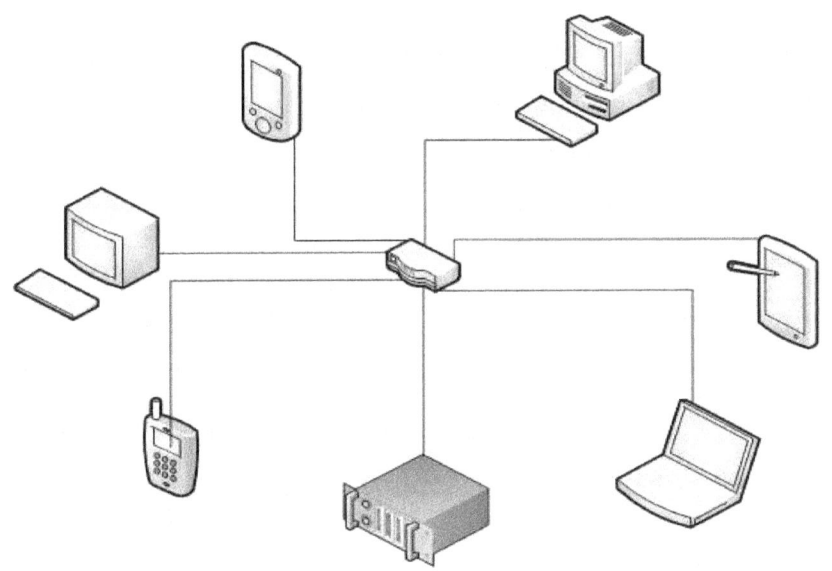

The communication between servers and clients

Services are generally involved with the abstraction of the resources of the computer. As such, clients are not really concerned with how the server works and performs to fulfill the request and deliver a response. What concerns the client is the response based on the application protocol.

A communications protocol defines the rules and language to be used, as explained above. The client-server protocols operate in what is called an application layer, which, in turn, defines the patters of the dialogue; further data exchange is formalized through the server's implementation of application programming interface. The API is a layer for accessing service and facilitates parsing by restricting communication to a specific format. Sometimes, a server may receive abundant requests in a short span. Normally, computers rely on scheduling systems to determine which requests from clients to accommodate first. Servers may provide limited availability by denying services to some clients. These types of attacks work by exploiting the server's process request obligations by overloading it with requests. An example of how client-server systems work is when an online banker accesses banking services through the web browser. The login credential of the customer is stored in the database, and the web server will act as an intermediary between the database server and client by accessing the database server. The application server responds to the data returned by applying the business logic of the bank and providing output to the web server, which will return the results to the web browser that is what the client sees. You notice that in each step of the sequence, there is a processing and requesting and returning data—the messaging pattern.

When explaining clients and servers, a related concept is a host. A host connects with other computers. A host is, therefore, a reflection of the logical relationship between computers on a network. To bring this concept to life in your mind, imagine that you want to download from another computer on the computer that you are using. The other computer is hosting the image and is, hence, referred to as the host computer. When a computer downloads pictures, for example, from other computers, the one that is being downloaded from becomes the host. Routers have the ability to host each other, and computers can do the same thing, too. However, a host must have an internet protocol address. Other components, therefore, do not qualify as hosts.

Server Access

Servers are connected either outside or within a local area network. Accessing a server will depend on whether it is a private or public internet protocol address. If the IP address is public, then it is possible to access it from the web. If, however, it is private, it can only be accessed from within the local area network. An alternative for accessing a private address would be to setup port, forwarding that allows remote access.

The speed at which data is retrieved from the server depends largely on the bandwidth required for data transfer. If the server is within the local access network, then the router determines how fast the data is transferred to the client from the server. You, therefore, need a quality router with high speeds. The logic applied for LAN network follows if the server is on the internet. Once you visit a webpage, the speed of the page load will depend on:

- The size of the webpage

- Speed of the website's server packets

- The bandwidth allowed by the ISP

- The speed of the router in routing data packets

Latency and bandwidth determine the performance experienced between clients and servers.

From the explanations above, it is logical to wonder if there is a difference between a server and the host. There are indeed differences, as the technology works differently from technology for sharing files. Usually, servers:

- Can be software programs or physical devices

- Provide specific services

- Are installed on the host computer

- Are of service to clients

Hosts, on the other hand:

- Are always physical devices or computers

- Serves multiple devices and users

The set-up shown below shows the server and clients and how they operate:

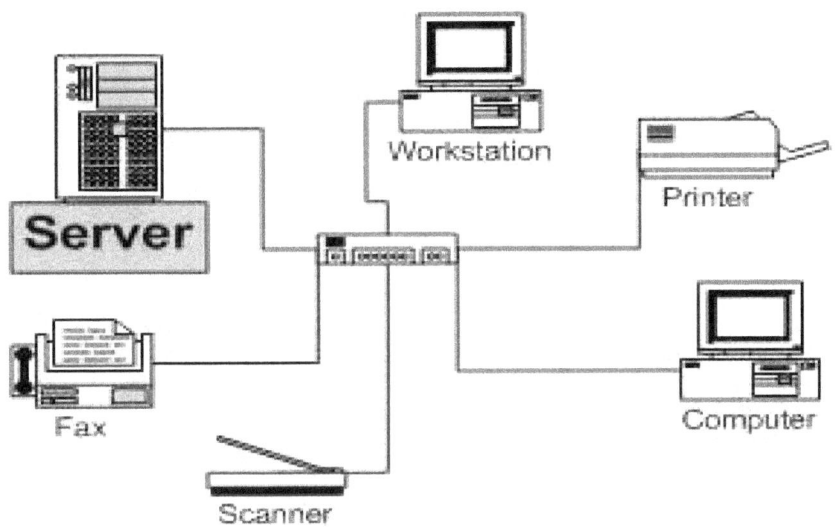

In this arrangement, you can see the server provides services to the rest of the machines on the network.

You have probably noticed that in the Windows workgroup environment, PCs within the network always have access to folders considered public on other computers within the environment.in the same light, it is not uncommon to find one computer hosting the media files of another because the former has a lot of space in the hard drive compared to the former. It is considered a host and not a server because, to be a server; the computer must serve only clients.

The advantage of using the workgroup in such a case is that it gives you easy access to media and any other files within the computers on your local area network. The disadvantage is that the files cannot be accessed beyond the LAN, and you can only access files if you have a server running on the host machine. Computers with static IP addresses can, however, function as servers with dual-purpose configuration.

Chapter 2: Network Topology

In simpler words, network topology involves the logical connection of computers within a network. It is the layout pattern of the computers and how they are interconnected within the network. It is the virtual structure or shape of the network. In topology, the devices found within the network are commonly referred to as nodes. Topology is, hence, depicted by showing the nodes and how they connect using cables. I will illustrate further below in what can be considered a logical explanation.

The network is crucial for the activities of an organization. Specific guidelines and models must be followed so that one device is connected to another. Below, we outline why network topologies are important:

- Topology plays an important role in network functioning.

- It plays a vital role in determining performance.

- It helps in creating an understanding of the concepts of networking.

- It helps in reducing the maintenance and operational costs, for instance, cabling costs.

- Network topologies make it easy to detect faults and errors within the network.

Physical and Logical Topologies

Logical and physical topologies are the basic categories in this kind of topology. The physical topology is the transmission layout that links devices. In fiber-optic mediums, physical topology involves cabling layout, node location, and the link between cabling and nodes. The topology of a network, in this case, is determined by the network access media and devices' capabilities, the level of fault or control tolerance desired and the cost of telecommunication circuits and cables. Logical topography, on the other hand, involves how signals act on network media. In simpler terms, logical topography is involved with how data passes from one device to the next in a network without regard to the physical interconnectedness of the device. The network's logical topography is not concerned with the physical, which means that they can be different within the same network.

Transmission media is also known as physical media. Transmission media is used to link devices that are within a network and includes:

- electrical cables

- radio waves

- optical fiber

Ethernet is a widely used physical media in the LAN network. Ethernet uses copper and fiber to transmit data. LAN standards use infrared signals.

Wireless Technologies and Wired Technologies

In the list below, the order of wired technologies is made from that with the fastest transmission speed to that with the lowest.

- **Optical fiber.** An optical fiber is a glass fiber that carries light pulses that represent data. There are advantages of optical fibers over metal wires that have low transmission and are always are not immune to electrical interference. This wired technology can carry multiple light wavelengths, which has a positive effect on the rate of data that can be sent. With optical fibers, you can send data at rates of up to trillions per second. This type of cable is needed for cables that carry high rates of data and are used to interconnect continents as undersea cables.

- **Twisted pair wires.** These are the most widely and commonly used medium for all telecommunication. They typically consist of a pair of copper wires twisted into one. They are used, for instance, in ordinary telephone wires. A normal telephone wire consists of a twisted pair, while Ethernet wires consist of copper cables that enable data and voice transmission. This improvisation of twisted wires is important because it helps reduce electromagnetic conduction and crosstalk. The transmission speed in twisted pairs can range between 2 million to 10 billion bits per second. They come in two forms: unshielded and shielded twisted pairs. Each of the forms comes suited and designed for used in different scenarios.

- **Ribbon cables.** The ribbon cable is popular as a cost-effective technology for serial protocols. They come in handy, especially over short distances and with lower data rates. They can be rolled within copper braids and within metallic enclosures.

- **Signal traces.** Signal traces are typical for board level serial communication and common in SPI.

- **Coaxial cable.** Coaxial cables are used for systems such as televisions. Usually, the cables are made of aluminum or copper that is insulated by a high dielectric constant material. This insulation is important for the minimization of distortion and interference. The transmission speeds for coaxial cables vary from 200 million bits per second to over 500 million bits per second.

Wireless technologies are quickly becoming common today. Below, we explain them.

- **Communications satellites**. These types of satellites communicate through microwave radio waves that do not get deflected on the atmosphere of the earth. Satellites are found in space, 22,236 miles above the equator in geostationary systems. These systems can relay and receive voice, TV, and data signals.

- **Terrestrial microwaves**. Terrestrial microwaves use special technologies that resemble dishes for outposts for communication. They are in the lower GHz assortment, which means all communications are limited to the lie of sight. The dispatch locations are placed about 30 miles apart.

- **PCS AND Cellular systems**. These systems utilize radio communication technologies. They divide a region that they cover into several geographic areas. Each geographic area then has a radio relay antenna device or lower power transmitter for relaying calls form an area to the next.

- **Free-space optical communication**. This type of technology uses both visible and invisible light for communication. They use the line of sight propagation to limit the physical position of the devices in communication.

- **Radio and spread spectrum technologies**. Wireless LANs make use of great occurrence hi-fi technology that is like low-frequency radio technology or digital cellular. This technology enables wireless LANs to enable communications between devices in a limited area. One of the common open-standards wireless radio-wave technologies is the Wi-Fi.

Chapter 3: Types of Network Topology and Network Administration

Physical and logical network topologies do not stop at that. Often, they can further be classified into five major models, as discussed below:

Bus Topology

To understand bus topology, consider the diagram below:

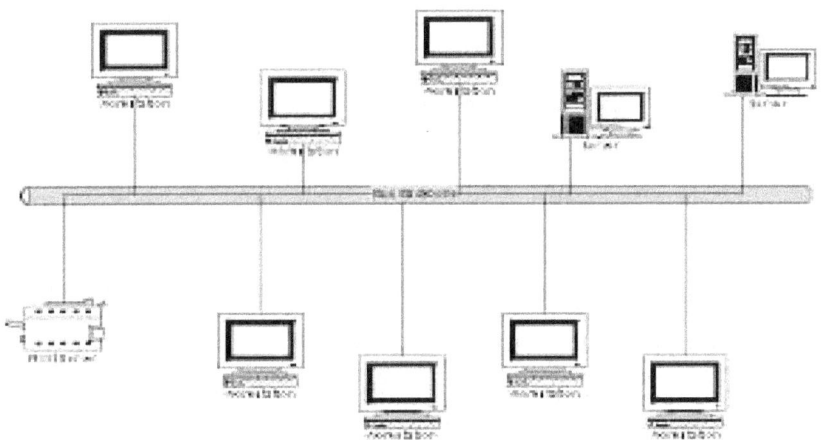

Bus topology is easily the most basic network setup for both logical and physical topologies. In this case, the devices and nodes are interconnected through the use of a single cable. In this type of topology, data is transmitted in one direction, and all devices are connected to a single cable. This simple setup is the reason that sometimes, this type of topology is referred to as backbone or line topology. A coaxial or RJ45 cable can be used to connect the devices in bus topology, depending on the devices and nodes. This main cable, therefore, acts as the network's backbone and one of the computers works as the server. The bus topology has advantages. First, it makes it relaxed to link a CPU or marginal device to the network. Also, it lowers the costs associated with cabling because the cable requirements are generally on the low compared to other topologies. Additionally, it is very easy to understand the bus topology due to its basic nature; it is an ideal type of topology for small networks, and it makes it easy to reduce or extend a network.

There are also disadvantages that come with the bus topology. While it can be ideal for small network setups, you may have to look elsewhere as the network becomes bigger. Also, if the primary cable fails, then the whole network will be affected, and it will fail as a result. Another disadvantage is the fact that the bus topology is unidirectional and that the speeds of transmission reduce greatly when the number of nodes increases. Also, compared to a ring topology, this kind of topology is slow.

Ring Topology

Ring topology can be understood from the next image:

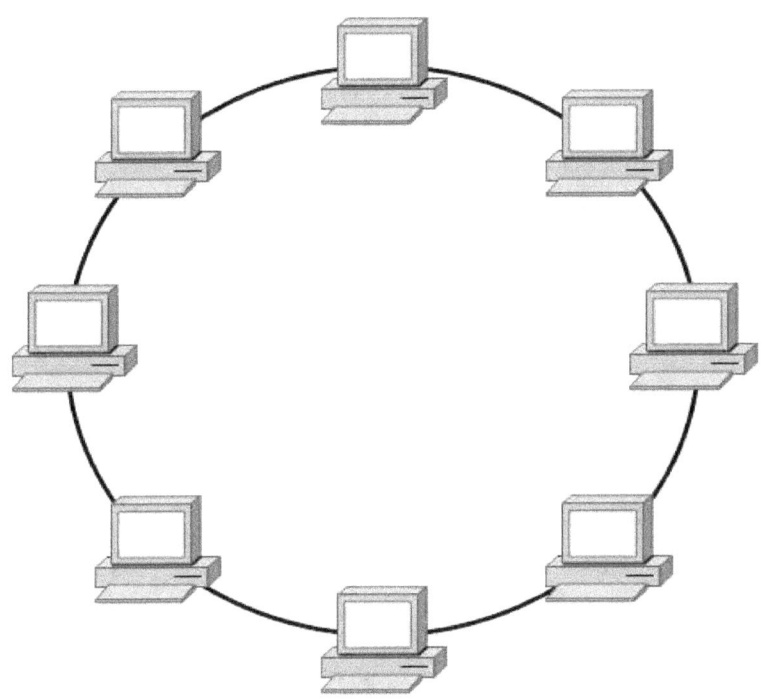

Ring topology is commonly called ring because the formation of a ring is evident as one computer connects to the next, and the last computer connects back to the first one. Each device has two neighbors, and the computers within the network form a circle as a result of their interconnection. Usually, one node within the network acts as a monitor that handles the configurations. Some of the features of ring topology include the use of repeaters for ring topology where a large number of nodes is involved. For instance, if someone wants to send information to the last node in a series of 100 nodes, then it has to pass through 99 others to reach the last, which presents the possibility of data loss. Repeaters are put in place to prevent loss of data within the network. Also, just like bus topology, transmission here is unidirectional. However, there is a possibility of making the transmission bidirectional by ensuring two connections between network nodes. When this is done, it is referred to as dual ring topology. What happens when this type of topology is introduced is that there are two ring networks in play, and data flow is in opposite directions to each other. This is advantageous because if one ring fails, the other ring comes in handy, acting as a backup that keeps the network up. In a ring topology, the transfer of data is sequential which, in this sense, means bit by bit. Data, therefore, pass through every node in the network and goes that way until it reaches the designated destination.

Ring topology is not just interesting but has advantages too. For instance, ring topology has the ability to maintain its speeds without slowing down, thanks to the fact that the transmission is not affected by the addition of nodes or high traffic. This happens because only nodes with tokens take part in data transmission. Also, this kind of topology is relatively cheap to install and easy to expand, making it a rival to bus topology when it comes to cost reduction. For ring topology, it assures better performance than bus topology, especially when the loads are heavy. Also, the point to point connectivity among nodes makes it a tad easier to know where faults and misconfigurations occurred, and it offers an orderly flow in the network.

Every good thing must have a disadvantage. Such is the case of ring topology. Some of the disadvantages of ring topology are the fact that it can be difficult to troubleshoot when a problem happens in the ring topology network. Also, network activity suffers a major blow should you try to add or delete computers from the network. Imagine a network of 100 computers and a possible disruption that requires you to remove two from the network. Also, if just one computer fails within the ring topology, it is bound to disturb the rest within the network. Also, there has to be a shared bandwidth among the devices within the network, and delays in communication are proportional to the number of nodes within the ring network. The more the nodes, the worse the communication delays will be.

Star Topology

Below is a picture that describes star topology

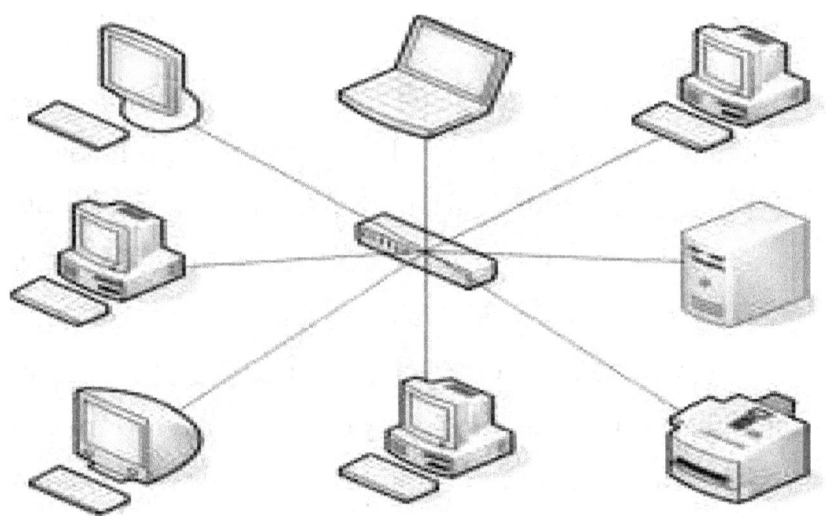

Just like the name suggests, star topology offers an arrangement where there is a central hub, which is a node or a computer which cares for the entire network and is surrounded by devices. They connect to the hub through a cable. In this arrangement, every node has a direct connection to the hub. Each of the devices within the network, therefore, has a direct connection with the central hub and the nodes have an indirect connection with the other nodes within the network through the central node. In star topology, data flows through the central hub before reaching the preferred destination. The central hub is, therefore, responsible for the control and management of data connectivity and transfer within the network. The central hub also has another role, the role of a repeater. A repeater, whose role is played by the central hub, ensures that there is minimal to no data loss when the transmission is taking place. To configure star topologies, coaxial or optical fiber wires are used.

There are advantages, as well as disadvantages associated with the use of the star topology. We begin with the advantages. One advantage of using star topology is that the failure of one node is inconsequential to the rest of the network as it is often not affected. Also, you can add remove, modify, and even possibly reconfigure devices without having to worry about disturbing the peace of the entire network. Another advantage that comes with this type of topology is the fact that you require minimum cabling for the configuration of the topology, and it is relatively easy to modify and even set up. When a problem occurs, it is equally easy to troubleshoot. On top of it all, there can still be fast performance even there is low network traffic, and there are a few nodes.

There are disadvantages, as well. For instance, there is the fact that the hub is the life of the entire network, and the network completely relies on it for survival. A failure in the hub means the failure of the entire network as the whole of it will be down. Also, unlike the topologies discussed so far, the star topology is expensive not only to install but to use as well. Most disadvantageous, however, is the fact that the network relies on the hub for configuration, efficiency, and even power.

Mesh Topology

Mesh topology is characterized by a point-to-point connection to other devices or nodes such that every node is connected to another within the network of computers (as shown below).

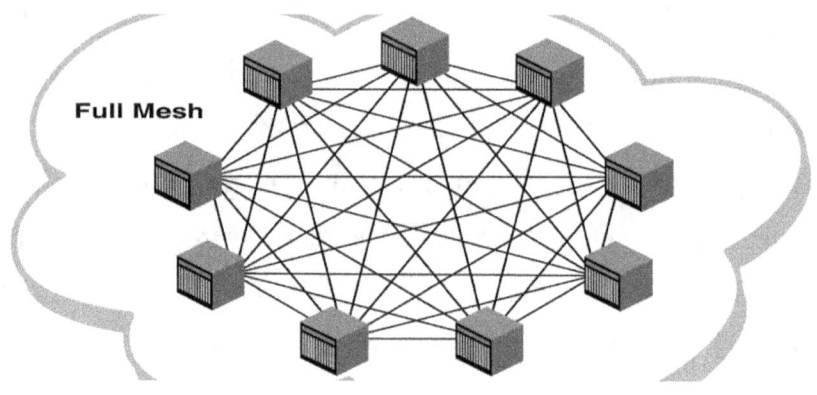

These node connections are not just direct but also non-hierarchical. Unlike the star topology, the network here is not dependent on one machine, and every node is active and playing a critical role in information relay. This type of topology is ideal ,especially in cases where there are workstations located in groups and when there is the use of a wide area network instead of the local area network. There are two vital techniques used to relay data in this type of topology.

- Routing

- Flooding

Routing involves making use of every node within the network such that every node in the network has a routing logic and data transfer is done through the routing logic. The routing logic is used as a tool to figure out the shortest route possible that can send information efficiently from the sender to the receiver. The trick is to use this logic to avoid broken data transmission lines.

Flooding involves transferring data to every node within the network. Here, there is no requirement for a routing logic as is required during routing. However, there are similar advantages here as no data is likely to be lost. In this case, this efficiency can be achieved because every node carries the same data within it. The network is, therefore, not only fault-tolerant but robust as well. Also, there is an increased load on the network as a result.

Just like the other topologies described above, the advantages and disadvantages of the mesh topology shall be discussed here. One interesting fact that also doubles as an advantage, in this case, is the fact that that the mesh topology is in actuality an extension of the star and bus topologies as addressed above. Also, another advantage is the fact that it is easy and very possible to expand nodes, while at the same time, the topology is easy to manage and maintain. It is also relatively easy to detect an error within the network with this type of topology.

There is also a high level of security and privacy associated with this type of topology, and the network is robust.

One disadvantage here includes the fact that the initial costs of installation and implementation can be high. It does not end there; the cost of cabling is high as well. For the untrained eye, mesh topologies can be difficult to understand. Another problem or disadvantage posed by this type of network is that installing and reconfiguring in a network that utilizes the mesh arrangement can be a big task. Also, with the presence of a central hub, the entire network is at risk should the hub fail.

Hybrid Topology

A hybrid topology typically consists of a mixture of two or more topologies. For example, one department within the office may utilize bus topology, another utilizes mesh topology, and the last utilizes ring topology. When these topologies are connected, they result in what is commonly known as a hybrid topology. Interestingly, with such a combination of topologies, it is certain that the hybrid kind of topologies inherits the advantages and disadvantages of the individual topologies that make it up. Usually, what determines the components of the hybrid topology is the fact that they are configured according to the requirements of the company. Therefore, the hybrid of one organization or company could easily differ from the next. With proper configuration, there is a likelihood that hybrid topologies provide an office with the best of all the topologies involved. The hybrid topology is illustrated below:

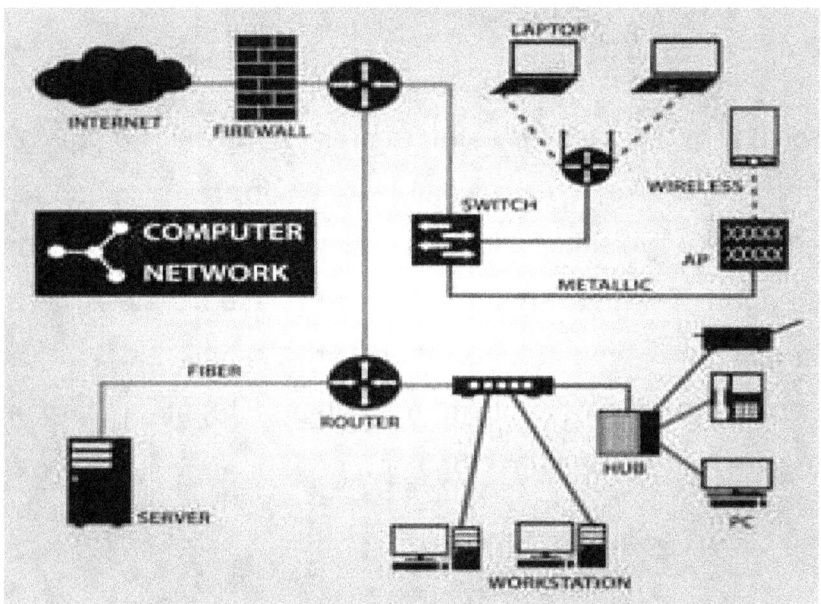

The advantages of hybrid topologies include the fact that they are reliable as it will be easy to troubleshoot and detect errors within the network. Also, as highlighted above, with proper connection, it is easy to get an effective network. The scalability of this type of topologies also gives it a competitive advantage compared to other types of topologies. Also, with different types of topologies in one, this topology is relatively flexible.

The disadvantages of hybrid topologies are few, including the fact that it is overly complex in design and can be costly during installation and even maintenance.

Tree Topology

The tree topology is considered a type of network topology by itself and yet, it qualifies as an exemplar of the hybrid topology. This is because it is a combination of the bus and star topologies. Typically, star topologies connect to each other within the network through the use of line topologies. There is a hierarchical type of connection between the nodes as they connect with each other, earning this type of topology its second name, which is hierarchal topology.

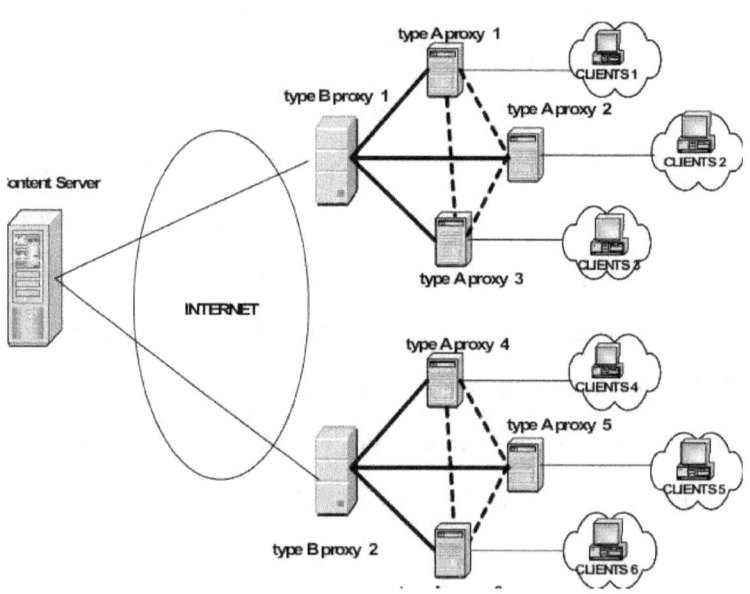

One of the major advantages that make this type of topology a favorite among many is the fact that it is highly flexible. In addition to flexibility, it is a scalable topology type as you can easily add or remove nodes according to your requirements and expectations of the network. Also, if you have a large network and have not quite figured out the right topology for you or your organization, then this may be it. With tree topology also comes the advantage in the ease of management.

There are a few disadvantages associated with a tree topology. For instance, the topology is definitely costly to install as a result of the robust cable work that will need to be done. Also, getting the right design to use after figuring out that the organization may need tree topology can be difficult. Maintenance costs that come with this type of topology can make it excruciatingly costly to maintain.

From the detailed explanation of the different topologies above, you will come to realize that choosing the right network may not be an easy job, but, it is possible when the right factors are put into consideration. These factors include the geographical distance between a node and the next, the number of nodes likely to be involved in the network, finances, and the flexibility in operation, maintenance, and many others that you may come across as you begin to figure out what may be the right fit for you. By now, you understand that, no one type of topology is fully superior to the next and that each has advantages and disadvantages that may come in handy when you are in the process of choosing. There is, therefore, no straight and correct answer or solution when you want to build and configure the right networking model for your organization or company, for instance. For any person thinking of adopting a topology, it may be wise to gather information and understand your needs and requirements before resting on a final decision for which topography will be best for you.

Chapter 4: Network Administration

By now, you must have understood that businesses, libraries, school, small, and even large corporations rely heavily on computer networks for the running of their day-to-day activities. It makes sense, in a world that is quickly becoming a global village to aspire for efficiency. This is where network administration comes in. In the midst of all these operations, there must be someone or even a group of people who are held account for the administration of these networks. The perfect word that can be used for this is network administrators. These very important people are the brains responsible for keeping the technology behind networks updated and ensuring that the networks run smoothly. This type of job is well-suited, especially with individuals who are technically inclined. However, it is important to realize that network administrators are, more often than not, critically skilled, and possess a combination of interpersonal skills, problem-solving skills, and technical skills. As a network administrator, you will not only interact with these machines but also with people, and, therefore, you need to have an understanding of the machines through technical and analytical skills and must be armed with interpersonal skills to maintain the human touch. It is a delicate play, but a lot of people have the right skills to help them get fully involved in network administration even as a career.

At this point, you may be wondering what the duties of network administrators are. We outline them below:

- Installation of hardware, including network printers, wireless access points, and video conferencing systems in an organization

- Deployment of upgrades and also enterprise applications

- Monitoring the network traffic of an organization to establish any suspicious activities and performance bottlenecks. Suspicious activities in such a case could include inappropriate network usage among employees and security breaches.

- Organizing, planning, and management of other administrators, especially as an administrator begins to climb higher up the career ladder

- Training the employees of an organization on the basics of networking and how they can handle user support calls

- Management of servers, mobile, and desktop equipment within the organization.

- In some instances, network administrators may work hand in hand with network architects in the designing and analysis of network models

- Supervision of computer support specialists

From the duties outlined above, it is clear to see why there is a need for the combination of technical and interpersonal skills when undertaking network administration duties. They require a deep knowledge of the technical world, and they should be able to quickly learn the details of server software and new networking packages. The role of network administrators is not always clear-cut, especially in small companies. In such settings, it is possible to find that the duties of the network administrator are pegged to those of network engineers. Also, sometimes, the terms system administrator and network administrator are used interchangeably as a result of related job roles in the two positions.

The responsibilities of network administrators fall within the four areas outlined below:

- **Designing the network.** Typically, this is the first phase of the life cycle of the network. While this is the initial phase of network administration, it is usually not carried out by new network administrators, as it can be a daunting task. This task will often involve making decisions on a variety of issues, for example, which network type best suits a given organization. In many large organizations, there is usually a senior network architect, basically a highly experienced network administrator that is familiar with the software and hardware of a network that will make decisions during the design phase of network administration. There are many factors involved in network design.

- **Setting up the network.** This is the step that comes after the initial design phase of network administration. This phase involves not just setting up but configuration of the network as well. If you are a network administrator, this is where you install any hardware that makes up the network's physical parts and configures databases, routers, hosts, and the servers for network configuration. This is a part played quite well by network administrators as the tasks within this phase are major responsibilities associated with the role of network administration. As such, as a network administrator in an organization, you should expect to perform these tasks unless the organization you work with is sufficiently large and with a system already in place.

- **Maintenance of the network.** After design and installation are done, the network must be maintained. There are many tasks that are involved in maintenance, including addition of new host machines to the network in question, administration of network services, such as name services and electronic mail and network security. Also, another duty is the troubleshooting problems within the network. These responsibilities constitute the bulk of duties performed by a network administrator in an organization.

- **Expansion of the network.** Sometimes, there is a need to expand existing networks. Interestingly, the more a network stays in place and functions efficiently, the higher the probability than an organization will need to expand its network's services and features. At the early stages, it is possible to expand the network by expanding network services and adding new hosts. However, over time, a network expands so much that further expansion will yield inefficient results. This is when the fourth phase of network administration comes into play. There are many different options available for this type of expansion, including the possibility of setting up a new network, then connecting it to the already existing network via a router, hence creating an internetwork. Also, it can involve configuring the machines in the office or even homes to remote networks thus enabling machines to connect to the network over social lines. Also, it may involve connecting the network to the internet so that those within it can retrieve information from the other systems, even when they are in different parts of the world. Lastly, a configuration can be done by configuring UUCP communications such that users can exchange files and emails through remote machines.

Principles of Network Administration

Administration of a network is done to ensure that it is under control in terms of resources and how they are utilized within the network. To maintain a network, there are principles that have to be followed and practiced. Below is an analysis of these principles:

- Firewall rules. A firewall ensures protection of an individual against threats within the computer network because it monitors all the traffic that comes in and goes out of the network, making a decision whether to permit or refuse it based on some set safety procedures. Firewalls have been the most popular and widely used line of defense in networking. They work by creating a barrier between untrusted outside sources, for example, the internet and internal networks that are trustworthy. Firewalls come as software, hardware, or both. There are various types of firewalls, including proxy, stateful inspection, unified threat management, next-generation, and threat-focused next-generation firewalls, all of which will be discussed in the later chapters of the book.

- VLAN management. The logical interface of a VLAN is known as the switched virtual interface. This interface is crucial in helping share resources and communication between layer three switches so that there can be inter-

VLAN communication. To create an SVI, you will initially have to create Layer 2 VLAN on a switch, after which you will assign an IP address on the Layer 3 VLAN interface. This Layer 3 will have an IP address just like physical routers. The difference, in this case, is that the third layer, in this case, is virtual. So, clients connected to the VLAN use the SVI interface as their gateway.

- Secure route configuration. To ensure a proper configuration of the router, there are several steps taken. For instance, there must be a change in the default username in the website of the router to ensure that the account information cannot be hacked. The SSID has to be changed and the MAC or physical address activated and the SSID broadcast feature disabled. Also, static IP addresses must be assigned, and the option for auto-connecting to Wi-Fi networks automatically must be disabled. Statistic IP addresses are then assigned to all devices in the network. Firewalls are also enabled to ensure security.

- Access control lists. Access control lists are typically catalogs of access control entries. Each access control entry identifies a specific trustee and specifies what rights are allowed and even denied for that specific trustee. There are basically two types of trustees, DACL and SACL. DACL is a discretionary access control list that identifies every trustee that is allowed or denied access to an object. When a procedure, therefore, attempts to gain admittance to a securable entity, the DACL comes into play, and the systems will scan the ACE to determine whether it should be granted permission or not. SACL is also known as the system access control list. It works by authorizing administrators who log on to try and reach a securable object. The log attempts of different administrators are itemized by every ACE, and therefore, a record in the security event log is generated.

Home Network Administration

Home network administration is just the same as professional network administration. As such, the duties of a network administrator in the workplace reflect what can be done in the home setting; the only difference is that it is done on a smaller scale. Some of the activities taken by home network administrators include:

- setting up broadband features with advanced features, such as QoS and wireless security keys

- troubleshooting performance issues and any outages that come within the network

- training family members on the technical details of network usage and network devices

- building a network backup system for the home

It is vital to realize that home networking cannot act as a substitute when it comes to network administration. However, when doing network administration in the home, you get a snippet of what network administration is all about. This educational value increases when you use your home networking expertise to help neighbors and friends with their network connection. For other people, network administration is a hobby that they love to undertake.

Building a Career in Network Administration

Computer networking is an attractive career that many have set their eyes on. It became a field of interest in the early 2000s and has not gone down the ladder of popularity since. The reason why computer networking continues to be popular is that there is a shortage of professionals that can take up jobs in the field, and yet, it can be an easy way for a person in the field to land a relatively lucrative position and scale-up in a fast-growing company. Whatever side of the debate you lie on, there are some things you should know about beginning a career in networking, expanding. Also, we outline some of the things you will need to be keen on when hunting for a job in this field. Luckily, these tips apply for other jobs in technical careers as well.

Job Titles in Networking

There are several positions when it comes to professional computer networking, and each of them comes with a variation in salaries and a high potential for long-term careers. The only disadvantage with this field is that job titles in networking can always be a source of confusion and not just for beginners but experienced people as well. There may be bombastic or bland titles that may fail to capture the essence of the actual work a professional may need to carry out in the field. There are some job titles that should be clearly spelled out as is done below:

✓ **Network administrator.** It is only fair, to begin with, that a large chunk of the discussion in the above sections has been focused on network administration. Basically, the job of a network administrator entails managing and configuring WANs and LANs.

✓ **Network engineer.** A network engineer is also called a systems engineer. The job role primarily focuses on system upgrades and evaluation of vendor products. Also, a systems engineer is always responsible for security testing.

✓ **Network technician**. Sometimes, network technicians are referred to as service technicians. The job, in this case, tends to give more focus on setting up, troubleshooting, and repairing both software and hardware products. It is not uncommon to find network technicians traveling to remote locations so they can upgrade fields and offer support as needed.

✓ **Network analyst**. A network analyst is also known as a network programmer. Their duties revolve around writing software scripts and programs that are useful in network analysis. Network analysis, in this case, involves monitoring of utilities and diagnostics. They also must evaluate third party products and integrate these products and software technologies into the already existing network environment. Conversely, they can easily build new network environments as well.

✓ **Network systems manager**. A network systems manager can also be called an information systems manager. Their main duties revolve around supervision of the work of network administrators, technicians, engineers, and programmers. They have a special focus on longer-range planning and make strategy considerations.

It is vital to realize that there are no uniform salaries in networking; in fact, salaries may vary, depending on different factors. These factors include which organization is in question, the market conditions within the locality, and the skill level and experience of the person being hired. This is why it is important to get into networking with a straight face and realistic expectations. Rarely will you find it a smooth walk in the park, but when you have the passion and determination for the job, you will find that your movement upward is a simple task. Advancement up the career ladder will often carry with it more lucrative opportunities when it comes to networking. Read on for more about gaining experience in networking.

Gaining Experience With Networking

Well, getting a job in networking can be quite an arduous task. This is because most employers are always seeking employees with experience, but where are you supposed to gain experience when you are fresh out of college? It is not uncommon to hear job seekers lamenting about this reality, and many people complain that the best and only way to gain experience is through getting hired. These sentiments may be true, despite the many promises of a lucrative job in the IT industry. The conditions are increasingly becoming harder and landing an entry-level position in networking can be difficult. However, you can still gain experience in other ways, as will be discussed in the next paragraphs. With these tips, you can have better chances of getting a good job and faster.

One great tip for gaining experience in networking is to pursue a help desk or programming internship full time in the summer months. Alternatively, you can take up a work-study job in these fields as they will work equally well. Internships are not assuring of the best pay, but the work could turn out to be more interesting or uninteresting for some. If the job is not interesting, there is a likelihood that an individual will not finish a substantial project during the limited time they have there. However, there is a clear advantage for you should you manage to complete your work-study or internship. Besides, you will gain hands-on experience, and you will be adequately trained, so you are ready for the market. With you being able to obtain and work well in these jobs, you demonstrate to your future and potential employers that you have an interest in the networking role you are applying for, and that is exactly what they like to see when hiring.

Another useful tip that can help you to gain experience is to self-study. Being handy can pay, albeit in different ways. One thing for sure, however, is that being hands-on can work in your favor as the skills you have can be useful and powerful when you demonstrate something to a potential employer. For instance, you may have just completed a class project recently. Do not stop there, extend the project in some way that will show that you can think out of the box, and show your abilities. You can also create a personal project that you have not been tasked to and complete it. A good way to start would be, for example, to experiment with network administration tools.

Also, earlier on, I mentioned something about home computer networking. This can be quite a useful way to gain experience. You can start with setting up the networks of friends and family and acting as an administrator for the same, for free. While this may not be the best idea for earning income, it will provide you with a basic understanding of how networks run. Should you find a job in business, however, remember that business computer networking is more complex. Therefore, you should expect that there is a different level of complexity and that you will use different technologies than you did in the home environment.

Also, the field of networking is vast and can be overwhelming for many people who may just be starting out. Instead of trying to eat more than you can chew by mastering every language and trying to keep up with every trend, make your life easier. Simply focus on the basic technologies that will be most important as you enter into the market. Over time, you will realize that you keep learning and keeping up if indeed, your interest is in the computer networking industry. Some core technologies that you can build expertise in include TCP/IP, as this will form a foundation for you to learn other specialized new ones in later life.

Education and Experience

As a person that is interested in venturing into networking, you may wonder the value that education holds when placed against the value of experience. As you may have noticed by now, a lot of employers seek out employees who have completed a four-year degree in university. This may not make sense in some instances, but it is important because they use this as a gauge for your commitment in the industry and field at large. The technology utilized in networking is not constant, and it keeps changing every other day. This is why employers find it important to know that you possess current information when it comes to networking and that you are willing to learn and adapt in the future as technology continues to change.

Certifications in networking help prove that you have the basic knowledge base, but college degrees are the real thing; they demonstrate your general ability to learn.

Experience is also important because it demonstrates that you have skills that are needed for the workplace. The more experience you have in the field, the better because it tends to put you in a better position to get a job. However, nothing beats the combination of experience and education when it comes to getting into networking as a career. This is because when you have both experience and education, it sets you apart from individuals who have one of each.

Representation of the Skills and Abilities

I discussed in the earlier sections that to get into network administration, a person should have a great combination of technical and interpersonal skills. I need to emphasize that interpersonal skills are important, and yet often, they are underrated. Also, you need to understand how to explain and exchange information pertaining to the technical aspects of networking. You will most likely be working in a team and not alone and having the ability to explain yourself verbally and in writing, both email and formal, you have the advantage of getting the chance to enjoy communicating with other networking professionals throughout your life as you seek to build your career.

Before even going further about the importance of communication skills at the networking workplace, let us start with the initial stages. You will definitely need good communication skills during an interview. Your ability to articulate yourself in the work environment is important, and the interviewers will be looking for possible clues into how well you can be understood within the networking environment as you work in a team. Therefore, understand the jargon used in such places and learn to relax when making conversation about such technical subjects. This is not something that will simply come to you in one day, but over time and with practice, you can learn so much that you can answer impromptu questions when asked. You can learn to articulate yourself through many tactics. For instance, you can visit local job fairs and discuss professional subjects with the people you will find there and with your friends. You will find that you gain indispensable knowledge on these subjects.

There are some tips that have been outlined above that may not work for people who are already in the field of networking. However, they can be used by those who aspire to venture into fields related to networking. Furthermore, there are tips that can be used no matter where you are in your career, for instance, visiting job fairs to help polish your skills. I hope that the information given can be of help to you, even in the slightest of ways.

Chapter 5: Network Infrastructure

Network infrastructure is part of IT infrastructure found within companies in enterprise IT organizations. Network infrastructure is interconnected and is usable for both internal and external communication. The network infrastructure in organizations is important because, in the digital age, the productivity and agility of a company are pegged on excellent equipment, as much as smart employees are also involved. For smooth running of operations, you require secure network infrastructure that will not let you down. Without the right infrastructure, you may find yourself suffering from security issues and poor user experience, which can impact the productivity of employees and customer experience and cost your brand its reputation.

It is, therefore, important that you and your organization understand how important network infrastructure is and be aware of the opportunities and possible challenges that come with network infrastructure. When you have the right knowledge of network infrastructure, you will be better placed to have maximum production and helping your organization reach optimum performance. Below, we dive deeper into the topic.

What Exactly Is Network Infrastructure?

The network infrastructure consists of resources needed to make the network work. These resources make network or internet connectivity, business operation, management, and communication within the organization possible. It consists of both software and hardware components, and it is what enables communication between services, uses, application, and processes and allows computing.

There is a common and interrelated term to network infrastructure. The term is IT infrastructure. In the simplest way, it is the same as network infrastructure. Interestingly, the terms are even used interchangeably and yet; there are ways in which they can differ subtly. IT infrastructure is used to define the large collection of elements of information technology that form the foundation for IT service. It encompasses the physical elements; in essence, the hardware and software components needed to form a healthy IT network. The network infrastructure, on the other hand, is seen as a smaller category compared to IT infrastructure. It is, therefore, as described before, a component of larger IT infrastructure. To have sustained success and cohesive solutions, a company should put in place both network and IT infrastructure. Below, the diagram expresses some of the components within a network infrastructure:

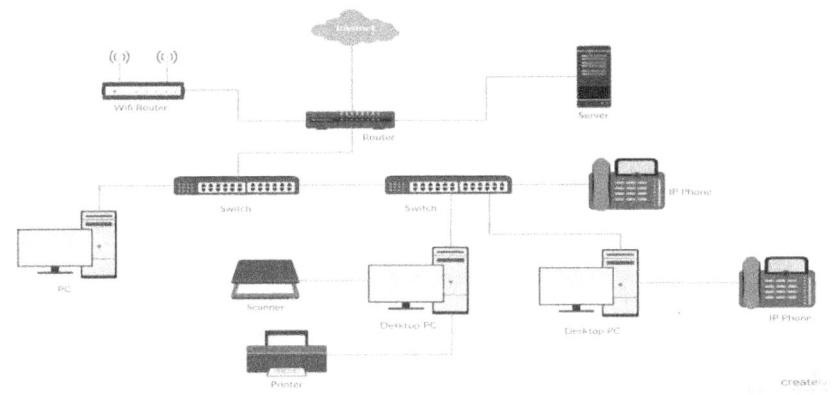

Why is network infrastructure important?

Network infrastructure is important because it can make or break a company and its reputation. It is, hence, important not only to have reliable IT infrastructure but also qualified personnel. These three components will work hand-in-hand to ensure a good and reputable company. The network is important mostly because it allows communication and connection. If there is no network infrastructure, other IT components such as software and hardware hardly make any sense and are not of much use. If, however, your network infrastructure is rich, clean, and secure, you are on your way to organizational excellence.

Challenges Surrounding Network Infrastructure

There are also challenges that surround network infrastructure that can prevent optimal functioning. Some of these challenges include:

- Centralization of traffic

- Duplication of data and how to deal with it

- Relaying the right data to the correct tool

Centralization of Traffic

An organization usually has several different locations or sites and subnets. If there is no centralized hub, it can be difficult to monitor and manage the network, and network visibility may also be an issue. Some companies have found a way around this, and typically, they use network infrastructure solutions to better understand what their network is and to centralize the heavy traffic. Infrastructure solutions also help companies to monitor and understand any data that traverses their networks. Using network infrastructure solutions, therefore, helps improve the security of a network and helps network operations teams address their issues with performance.

Data Duplication

Data duplication is also a major issue when it comes to network infrastructure. In Extreme instances, duplication can occur for up to 50 % to 66 % of network traffic. Duplicate data may present problems, especially with regards to network security solutions. If network security solutions encounter a lot of duplicate data, there are new risks involved. First, the duplicate data makes the solutions slow down, and eventually, they are not able to detect threats within the network infrastructure. Removing duplicate data is, therefore, not just important but critical for the well-being of the organization as well.

Relaying the Right Data to the Correct Tool

Different organizations use a variety of different cybersecurity providers and tools. These security providers charge organizations based on the amount of data they need to process. It is, therefore, important that the data sent is relayed to the right tool. If data is sent from various sources to one and the same tool, it may end up not only being ineffective but also costly, especially in a case where one tool suits a different type of data than another one.

There are solution providers that help organizations and companies to keep an efficient, clean network, as this work is not a small task. It may, therefore, be helpful to have a team with deep security and networking expertise in your organization. Unlike in the past, where network infrastructure was clear cut, today, the network infrastructure field is dynamic and complex, with a mixture of cloud and on-premise management. Even when on-premises networking happens, it is possible for a company to have a mix of vendors and networks. When companies merge, and when there is organic growth, there tends to be further mix up in the network infrastructure, which eventually, ends up having a negative impact on network infrastructure. When such eventualities come about, sometimes companies end up with up to five tools for monitoring and managing what is now a hybrid network. If you want to have your company and network safe and performing at its peak, this may not be the best or ideal environment. You may need to establish a central hub where you can view all your network traffic and get the tools to direct the right traffic to the right tools.

Network visibility remains important mainly because the good performance of a company relies mainly on the infrastructure and its ability to monitor performance and detect threats. If a company is able to deal with network blind spots, then they are able to uncover the blind spots, identify threats from the sources uncovered, and remediated solutions quickly. With these solutions in place, it is possible for the organization to remove duplicate data and allow for efficiency in the network and security tools.

Network Protocols and Standards

The definition of terms is important in networking. From the above sections, we have had a step-by-step development of concepts that have so far given an idea of how networks function. Now, the reader is going to be introduced to network protocols, what standards are, and what role they play in networking.

Network protocols are the policies and standards, including formats, rules, and procedures that define how two or more devices communicate over a network. These protocols govern end-to-end processes and ensure that data and network communication is secure and also timely. Protocols include all the requirements, processes, and restraints involved in initiating and accomplishing communication when it comes to servers, computers, and other devices within the network. Protocols have to be affirmed and installed by both receivers and senders so that data and network communication is possible and to ensure the application of software and hardware nodes that do the communication over a network.

There are types of network protocols:

- Network communication protocols, such as HTTP and TCP/IP

- Network security protocols, such as HTTPS, SFTP, and SSL

- Network management protocols, including SNMP and ICMP

It is important for anyone who is seeking to understand networking to understand network protocols. This information is usually key to understanding communication and troubleshooting communication problems within networks. Also, these network protocols give the network devices a common language through which they can communicate. Without protocols, therefore, computers cannot achieve communication with each other. Network end users heavily rely on these network protocols to connect.

How Do Network Protocols Work?

You may be wondering how network protocols work. In the simplest terms, these protocols work by breaking down what are seemingly large processes into narrowly definite, more discrete tasks across each level within the network. In a standard model, the Open Systems Interconnection model, there are network protocols that govern the activities in each layer in the exchange.

A protocol suite is a set of network protocols that work together. The TCP/IP suite is a type of suite that includes a number of protocols across layers. These work together to enable internet connectivity. The network protocols involved include:

- **User Datagram Protocol.** This protocol is simply referred to as UDP and takes the responsibility of acting as an alternative protocol of communication to the transmission control protocol. UDP is used in establishing loss-tolerating and low-latency connections between the internet and various applications.

- **Transmission control protocol**. Also known as TCP, this control protocol uses rules that have already been set to ensure communication exchange between internet points in information packets.

- **Internet protocol**. Also known as IP, this protocol uses rules that have been set to receive and send messages based on the internet address level.

- **Other network protocols, including hypertext transfer protocol and FTP**. These protocols have defined a set of rules that help in the exchange and display of information.

All packets that are transmitted and received within a network have binary data. Usually, a packet will have a header at the beginning of a packet. This header stores information regarding the sender and the intended destination of the data. Some packets also have footers at their end, and they contain additional information about the sender and destination. The network protocols involved then process the headers and footers and sieve messages of each kind as they move among devices. There are groups that set up these industry standards and publish them.

Network Communication Protocols

Communication protocols include formal descriptions of rules and digital message formats that are required during the exchange of information between and in computing systems and devices and in telecommunications at large. Communication protocols cover a wide range of processes, including error detection, authentication, and signaling and error correction. These protocols also describe the synchronization of digital and analog aspects of communication, semantics, and syntax. These protocols are implemented in both hardware and software, and it is not surprising that there is an abundance of communication protocols used in both digital and analog communications. In short, computer networks cannot be existent without communication protocols. The properties of transmission that a protocol is able to define include transmission size, packet speeds, techniques of synchronization and handshaking, types of correction errors, sequence control of packets, address formatting, routing and address mapping. Some well-known communication protocols are Hypertext Transfer Protocol (HTTP), Simple Mail Transfer Protocol (SMTP), User Datagram Protocol (UDP), File Transfer Protocol (FTP), and Internet Message Access Protocol (IMAP).

Where digital computing systems are involved, the rules of the communication protocols are expressed by data structures and algorithms. Protocols, therefore, serve the same purpose to communication as algorithms and programming do to communications. Operating systems contain processes that cooperate and manipulate data that is shared so that they connect with each other. The connection is usually guided by protocols that can be entrenched within the very course. There is no shared memory, and so, the systems that are communicating have to do so using s common transmission medium. Transmission is such a case is not fully reliable, and there may be the use of different operating systems and even hardware.

For the successful implementation of a networking protocol, the software models have to be interfaced with the machine's operating system's framework that has already been implemented. The framework is responsible for the implementation of networking as a functionality in the operating system. Protocol algorithms are articulated in what is a transferable language in programming, and the protocol software becomes independent of the operating system. Some of the well-known frameworks are the OSI model and the TCP/IP models.

When the internet was developed, the successful design approach for both operating systems and compiler was abstraction layering. A remarkable resemblance between programming languages and communication protocols exists, which is the reason that the original monolithic schmoosing plans were disintegrated into liaising protocols. Eventually, this contributed to the upsurge of the layered protocol perception, which, today, is the center of protocol design. Typically, systems cannot utilize a solitary protocol for broadcast. As an alternative, systems utilize collaborating protocols, which has been described above as a protocol suite. Protocols are arranged according to their functionality in clusters, for example, a cluster of the transport protocol. In this case, functionalities are plotted into layers, and each layer solves a specific type of issue. For transmission of a message, protocols are selected from every layer. The next protocol is accomplished through the extension of the message with the next layer's protocol selector.

There are other basic requirements needed in this process, and getting files transverse the network is only a small fragment of the protocol. When files are acknowledged, it is evaluated so that the context of progress within the conversation is established. The protocol, then, contains guidelines that describe the context as well. The syntax of communication is expressed through the rules of context. There are other rules that express the semantics of communication. To begin communication, the communication systems facilitate the sending and receiving of messages. Thus, protocols govern the rules of transmission, while the following must be adhered to:

✓ Data formats that will enable records interchange

Bit-strings of digital messages are exchanged and divided into fields such that a field will carry only material pertinent to the protocol. The bit-string is usually separated into the payload and header. The payload carries the message while the header has information pertaining to the protocol operation. If a bit-string is longer than the SMTU, then it is divided into pieces that are of the right size.

✓ Address mapping

In some instances, protocols are required to map addresses of a particular scheme on those of another. For instance, for an Ethernet MAC address application to translate a specified logical IP address, it has to map addresses.

✓ Address formats for data exchange

Addresses exist solely for the purpose of identifying senders and recipients. Bit-strings contain headers that carry addresses, allowing for the receivers to resolve if the bit-strings are appropriate, thus must be processed or if they must be ignored. The connection between the receiver and sender is identified using what is known as an address pair. Address values, sometimes, consist of special meanings. For instance, if an address is comprised of all -1s, then it can be supposed that it is addressing every station of the network and the message shall be broadcast so that the entire local network receives it. The rules that are used are referred to as addressing schemes, which determine the meanings corresponding to the address values.

✓ Routing

Routing typically happens when systems do not have a direct connection with each other. Intermediary systems are, therefore, needed to send messages in place of the source along the route, which are called "routers." The way the routers connect through routers on the internet is known as internetworking.

✓ Detecting transmission errors

If there is a possibility of data corruption anywhere within a network, then it is necessary that errors are detected and eliminated as soon as possible. Usually, the CRCs of any data are attached to the packet's end, and this makes it possible for whoever is receiving the data to detect corruption in it because they can see the differences. In such a case, the receiver rejects the packet-based in these CRC differences and makes arrangements for fresh transmission.

✓ Time outs and retries causing loss of information

Sometimes, packets may be delayed in transit, or they may be lost on the network. To deal with such issues, some senders who are operating under protocols can expect that the receiver acknowledges that they received the correct information within a relatively short time. When, therefore, there is a timeout, the receiver may need to inform the sender who retransmits the information. In the case where links are permanently broken, there is really no need for retransmission, so the number of retransmissions is usually limited. If the limits for retrying are limited, then what occurs is an error.

✓ Flow control

The importance of flow control resides on the sender's task of transmitting data fast—faster than what the receiver's network equipment can actually process. It is, however, possible to control flow by messaging to the sender.

✓ The direction of the flow of information

If transmissions can only occur in one direction at a time, as transmission happens on half-duplex links, then there is a need to address transmission direction. Arrangements are made to accommodate contention, like in a situation when two parties concurrently need to transfer data.

✓ Control of sequence

As we explained above, bit-strings may sometimes be divided into pieces. When this happens, the pieces of bit-string sent on the network may get delayed or get lost completely. Sometimes, they may end up taking different routes to their destination and what results is that the bit-strings arrive out of sequence. Resubmission, on the other hand, can result in pieces that are duplicate. However, it is still possible to mark pieces with sequence information such that the receiver is able to determine what was duplicated or lost and ask for retransmission where information was lost. It also becomes possible to reassemble what could have been the original message.

Protocol Design Principles

Network protocol design principles have been based on systems engineering principles. Therefore, to design complex protocols, decomposition into smaller cooperating protocols is necessary. Operating systems operate synchronously. The synchronization of software is a primary aspect of concurrency in programming. This receives and sends communication in the right sequence. This type of programming, when it comes to operating systems theory, has always been a topic among programmers. If carefully studied, you will realize that there are several analogies between programming and communication. In such a case, the CPU is likened to a transfer mechanism of a protocol.

Below, I introduce the rules that allow programmers to design protocols that are independent of each other but can cooperate.

Layering

Protocols are layered in modern protocol design so that they can form a protocol stack. Layering comprises a design principle that splits the protocol into smaller phases that complete specific parts while interrelating with the protocol's other areas in minor but well-defined means. The layers have a role of testing and designing independently the protocol's various parts, thereby eradicating the chances of combinatorial explosion while keeping the designs simplistic.

The internet's communication protocols are supposed to function in, not only complex but also, diverse settings and are designed for modularity and simplicity, and they fit into the hierarchy of layers as defined by the internet protocol suite. TCP and IP, the first two protocols that cooperate come as a result of decomposing the original TCP into a layered suite of communication.

Another protocol is the seven-layered model or the "OSI model." This was developed for general communication as a reference model. The difference is that this layer has a more rigorous concept of functionality and stricter rules of protocol interaction. Application software is always built on a strong transport layer the routing mechanism, and datagram delivery underlies the transport layer. The routing mechanism is connectionless when it comes to the internet. Network link technologies are the layer on which packets relay upon networks. Network link technologies include Ethernet which is physical layer technologies. Layering allows the exchange of technologies when necessary; for instance, to accommodate the connection of networks that are not similar, protocols can be stacked in a tunneling arrangement.

Protocol layering is, hence, the basis for protocol design. Protocol layering allows the decomposition of complex protocols into simplistic ones that can cooperate. Also, since every protocol goes into a protocol layer, this can be seen as functional decomposition. Each distinct protocol layer has distinct problems related to communication. The IP suite consists of internet-network and application-transport functions. Together, they make up a layering model or layering scheme.

Network architecture and protocol layering design are interrelated, so they have to be designed alongside each other. The features of these two in relation to each other are as described in the next paragraphs:

The internet is a source of universal connection. Any two computers that connect to the internet can, therefore, communicate. All computers on the internet are identified by an internet address and reach the user as one huge network composed of interrelated physical networks. This is what we know as the internet, which is a system of interconnection that is also known as "internetwork."

Internet addresses consist of the host-id and net-id. The host is identified by the hosted, while the network is identified by the net-id. The term host can mislead, as often, a computer may have multiple work interfaces, and each will have its own unique address. The internet address, on the other hand, does not identify a connection to one computer but rather to the network. This is the id that is used by routers to determine where a packet should be sent.

Routers ensure the interconnection of physical networks. They forward packets that appear between the interconnected networks and make it possible for one host to reach another when on a physical network. There is a flow of communications between two systems that communicate through routers, and datagrams are delivered from router to router until one that can deliver the datagram to the attached network is reached. A routing table is consulted in the case where a decision has to be made, whether a datagram needs to be sent to a router closer to the destination or it can be delivered directly to the network. The routing table typically consists of paths and networkids that need to be followed to reach a network. The path prescribed is, therefore, either direct (there's a sign that the datagram can be brought straight to it) or not (there is an alternative route that is closer to the destination).

All networks, be it WAN, LAN, or point-to-point links, are treated as the same network.

The internet offers a packet-switched system that adapts well to a range of hardware, including Ethernet. Connectionless delivery involves streams and messages being allocated into pieces and are multiplexed on high-speed interconnected machines that allow simultaneous use of connections. The divided pieces each carry information that helps identify what the destination is. The delivery is, however, unreliable, as sometimes, packets get lost, delayed, delivered despite defect, or duplicated without warning to either the source or receiver. This unreliability comes as a result of a shortcoming in which the underlying networks fail, or resources are exhausted. The internet protocol defines an unreliable connectionless system. Also, the routing function is specified by the IP protocol. Virtual circuits between senders and receivers are built up through connection-oriented systems. Once virtual circuits are built up, datagrams are sent like any other data through virtual circuits. This data is forwarded to IP protocol modules.

The transmission control protocol defines a reliable stream transport service. These services are layered; on top are the application programs, also called "application services," which can utilize the transmission control protocol. Should the program interrelate with the packet delivery system, the process takes place through the user datagram protocol.

Software Layering

Software layering/design is done after the protocols, and protocol layering has been established. Software is layered in an organization and has a relationship with protocol layering. To send messages on a system, the modules have to interact such that the top one interacts directly with the one below it. It then hands over the message for encapsulation. The module establishes a reaction, which is encapsulating the data presented within its data area and filling the header with the data according to the protocols. To interrelate with the module right beneath it, it passes over the newly compiled information where it is appropriate. The module at the bottom directly interacts with the module at the bottom of the next receiving system such that the message gets sent across. The reverse happens on the receiving system such that the message is eventually delivered to the destination in its original form if, by good luck, it does not experience any protocol violations or transmission errors.

When it comes to protocol errors, the delivering module discards any received pieces and hands to the source of the piece on the same layer, the report of an error condition. It does this by dispensing an error message below or delivering it across, in the case where there is a bottom module. The layer that introduced division and reassembly handles the stream of data and division of the messages into pieces, and their final reassembly is done at the final destination. The translation of programs is divided into the following:

- Loader

- Compiler

- Link editor

- Assembler

This signifies the layering of the translation or software, which allows them to be designed independently. The complexity of program translation could be conquered in some ways, and these ways could be applied to protocols; the brains behind the TCP/IP protocol suite ensured that they imposed the same layering when it came to software frameworks.

Strict Layering

Strict layering involves adherence to a layered model. However, this cannot be considered an ideal method of networking since strict layering typically can cause severe effects on the performance of a system. There must, therefore, be a trade-off between performance and the simplicity offered by layering. Researchers criticize the rather widespread use of protocol layering for the primary reason of having a probability of duplication between a higher layer and a lower layer's functionality.

Protocol Development and the Need for These Standards

Protocols have the selected standards for communication to happen ultimately. Rules are expressed through data structures and algorithms. The operating system and hardware are independent, and this is enhanced by the expression of the algorithms into what is a portable programming language. The standards of protocol are achieved by obtaining the support and, ultimately, approval of a standards organization. The standards organization is responsible for protocol development. An agreement is created for the organization's members to adhere voluntarily to the result of the work. Often, these members control the larger market shares relevant to protocols, and the standards are reset by the government because they also serve an important public interest. Sometimes, they do not gain enough acceptance, and the government or law has to come in disclosing the source code and enforcing it for the sake of the public.

To further enhance an understanding of the importance of these standards, you can take the example of IBM's bi-sync protocol. This early link-level protocol was for use in correcting two nodes that were separate. When it was used in a multimode network, some deficiencies were realized. Manufacturers and organizations can enhance the protocol as they see fit in the absence of standardization, and this has led to the creation of versions that are even incompatible on networks. Today, there exists over 50 variants of the BSC, something that could have been stopped by the presence of standardization.

Sometimes, protocols fail to go through the standardization process and yet still gain dominance in the market. The protocols, in this case, are called de-facto standards. De-facto standards tend to be a common trend in monopolized markets, niche markets. Sometimes, they are used to scare away competition, and this can have a negative impact on the market. Standardization is, therefore, a way to counter-act de-facto standards and their ill results. However, de-facto standards are not always negative. In some instances, such as the case of GNU/Linux, there is no undesirable control on the market. The reason for this is that the sources are published and maintained openly, which invites the existence of competition. The solution for open systems interconnection, therefore, does not have to be standardized.

Chapter 6: Network Protocols and Standards

Network Protocols

Network protocols in the simplest sense are the policies and standards, including but not limited to, the formats, procedures, and rules that define how devices, two or more, communicate within a network. These policies and standards govern the end-to-end processes involved in communication and ensure timely, secure delivery of data, and network communication. Protocols in a network incorporate the processes, constraints, and even requirements of accomplishing communication between servers, routers, computers, and other devices that may be network-enabled. Normally, these network protocols are installed and confirmed by the receivers and senders so that network and data communication is done, and they apply to both the hardware and software nodes that communicate with each other on a network.

As such, a protocol can be likened to the language through which communication happens on the internet. This is because there is a set of mutually accepted rules that are also implemented as both ends of what is perceived to be the communication channel to ensure proper communication exchange. Two devices can exchange information only if they adopt the rules. We, therefore, cannot even dare communicate over the internet without the use of protocols. Every protocol is defined using unique terms, and each has a different name. Typically, messages travel from the sender to the receiver through a medium just like normal communication does. In this case, the medium refers to the physical path over which the information will travel once it is sent and expected by the receiver. It uses a protocol.

These formats are used among communicating systems to exchange messages, where each has a precise meaning and is intended for a particular recipient. This recipient then produces a singular response from a pool of all probable responses predetermined for the specific situation being examined. This characteristic is typically autonomous of its intended implementation communication protocols agreed to by the parties involved, and to do this, protocols are developed according to technical standards. This kind of arrangement is also the same for a programming language, and it can, therefore, be said that protocols act to communication as programming languages do to computations. Different protocols describe different aspects of communication. A group of protocols that have been designed to work in collaboration is known as protocol suites. When protocol suites are implemented in software, they are known as protocol stacks. The Internet Engineering Task Force publishes internet communication protocols, and hence, it handles both wired and wireless networking that has become a prominent part of present-day networking. The International Organization for Standardization, also known as ISO, on the other hand, handles other types of networking. Yet another organization, the ITU-T, handles protocols for telecommunications and public switched telephone network (PSTN) formats. This and internet coverage are uniting over time. As such, the standards are doing the same and are moving towards convergence as well.

Communicating Systems

Between other media and the devices in a network, communication is exchanged in every instance. This type of exchange is administered by predetermined agreements set out in communication protocol specifications. These specifications work to define the state-dependent behaviors, actual data that is exchanged, and the nature of communication. Digitally, in computing systems, the rules are expressed as data structures and algorithms, while in communication, they are expressed as protocols. Operating systems, which we will discuss later in the book, usually contain cooperating processes that work to manipulate the data that has been shared within devices to know what was being communicated. The protocols that govern this communication and protocols are also embedded in the process code. Communicating systems do not have shared memory, and therefore, they have to use a shared transmission medium for communication with each other. Transmission as the way to achieve the ultimate goal of communication may not be reliable. As such, individual systems sometimes end up using different operating systems and different hardware. When implementing a network protocol, software modules for protocols and frameworks within the operating systems of machines interface. The framework is responsible for implementing the operating system's networking functionality. Protocols are usually expressed in portable programming language, and when this happens, protocol software and the operating system are made independent of each other. The TCP/IP and OSI models are the most popular frameworks.

A design approach that has been deemed successful is abstraction layering from the days as early as when internet development was taking place. Abstraction layering was a useful design approach for both the operating system and compiler design. There are similarities between communication protocols and programming languages, and this meant that the monolithic networking programs could be broke down into protocols that could work together, giving rise to the concept of layered protocols. As a result of such developments, today, layered protocols are the basis of protocol design. One protocol is generally not enough for systems when transmitting information. Instead, there are sets of protocols that cooperate to ensure transmission, and they are known as protocol suites. Protocols are arranged based on the way they function in groups. To illustrate, take a group of transport protocols, for example. Here, the groups of layers pertain to certain functionalities, where each of the layers solves a particular class of problems that relate to different aspects, such as internet, application, transport, and network functions. For a message to get transmitted, each layer gives a chosen protocol. The subsequent protocol's selection is attained when the message is drawn-out by a protocol selector in each of the layers.

Basic Requirements for Network Protocols

For data to get across, an entire network is just a small part of the equation when it comes to transmission. Once the data is received, more things happen. For instance, data has to be evaluated so that it can be understood how far the conversation has reached. Protocols, therefore, must be inclusive of rules of engagement that will describe the context. The rules in question express communication syntax. There are other rules as well, and these ones determine the usefulness of the data that has been transmitted according to the context of the exchange. They are the rules that express the semantics of communication. Communication, in this case, involves semantics and syntax.

There is the sending and receiving of data on communication systems, and protocols define and specify the rules that are responsible for the government of transmission. The aspects described below are, therefore, to be addressed

Data Formats for Exchange of Data

In this sense, there is an exchange of information bit-strings. There is a division of the bit-strings into fields, and every one of these fields carries information that is relevant to the protocol in question. There is a division in the bit-string, so it consists of two parts: the payload and header. The payload is responsible for carrying the actual message, and the header, on the other hand, is responsible for fields that are relevant to the protocol's operation. There is a maximum transmission unit for bit-strings, and sometimes, some bit-strings are longer than this specified minimum. In such cases, the bit-strings end up being divided into smaller appropriate-sized pieces.

Address Formats for the Exchange of Data

Addresses in networking are just like addresses for humans in real life. They identify who the sender of information is and who the intended receiver is. The header area in the bit-string described above contains this information, and this allows the recipients of the message to determine if the bit-strings will be of use to them or not so that they can process or ignore the message therein. There may be a connection between the receiver and the sender, and this is identified using what is known as an address pair. Address pair come with values that have meanings for the receiver and sender. Sometimes, the addresses come with special values that have meaning. This is what results in a broadcast message in a local network. An address scheme is the set of rules that describes the meanings of the address values in the address pair.

Mapping of Addresses

This happens when protocols need to address one scheme to another. For example, when there is a need to translate an application specified logical IP address to an Ethernet Mac address, address mapping must happen so that the address of the first scheme is understood to the second scheme.

Detection of Errors That Occur During Transmission

Data detection is a necessary and important part of the process of data transmission in networks. It is especially necessary in cases where data corruption has occurred. The most common approach to this issue is the attachment of CRCs to the end of packets. When the CRCs are added, then it is possible for the receiver of data to establish that there are some differences that have occurred as a result of corruption. This gives the receiver a basis for rejecting the packet, and therefore, arrangements are made for retransmission.

Routing

Sometimes, you may find that systems do not connect to each other directly. In such cases, there is the employment of intermediary systems that work to connect the intended receiver with the message. These routers forward the message on behalf of the sender and make it possible for the receiver to get the intended message. "Router" is a term that is used when these connections happen on the internet, and the resulting interconnection of networks is referred to as internetworking, as mentioned earlier.

Acknowledging

When there is the expectation of communication, then acknowledgment that the correct data was received is necessary. The receiver usually sends the acknowledgment to the original sender of the message.

Timeouts and Retries

Interestingly, despite taking all the necessary precautions, packets tend to be lost in networks sometimes. At other times, there may be a simple delay in the delivery of the packets. This is where acknowledgment plays a role because the sender expects that the receiver sends an acknowledgment so that they are sure that the message was received. The acknowledgment is expected in a set amount of time, and this gave rise to the concept of timeout. When the time lapses and the sender has not received an acknowledgment, it becomes a cue that there is a need to retransmit the information. In other cases, links may permanently be broken. In such cases, retransmission usually loses its effect, resulting in a restricted number of retries. When number of retries exceeds that of the limit, then an error follows.

The Direction in Which Information Flows

Sometimes, transmissions occur in one direction as would be on the case of information that flows from one sender at a time or half-duplex. If this happens, then there is a problem that will need to be addressed. This is the root of the concept of media access control as arrangements are made so that the case of contention and collisions are involved. Collisions happen when two senders want to simultaneously send out information, and contention happens when the two senders both wish to transmit data.

Control of Sequences

As we had discussed above, sometimes, bit-strings may need to be transmitted after division into smaller pieces. However, problems may arise as most times, when these bit-strings are sent individually on the network, they may get delayed and sometimes, lost as they may take different routes to reach their destination. In such cases, these pieces of bit-string end up reaching the destination out of sequence. Retransmissions, on the other hand, will result in duplicate pieces, which does not solve the problem. As such, the pieces are marked with sequence information when they are still with the sender. If, therefore, they reach the receiver when out of sequence, the receiver has the right tool to determine what is duplicated and can know what was lost and either reassemble or ask for retransmission as is best seen.

Control of Flow

The flow needs to be controlled when the sender is transmitting packets of data faster than can be received and processed by the intermediate network or receiver. As we have mentioned earlier, the best way to establish flow control is by messaging the sender and receiver.

Design of Protocols

To generate a group of common principles governing protocol design for networks, the system engineering principles have been put into use. Therefore, to design complex protocols, it is necessary to decompose simpler protocols that can cooperate within the conceptual framework. There is a concurrent type of operation in communicating systems. Synchronizing the software that receives and transmits messages in proper sequences is an essential part of this type of programming. Traditionally, concurrent programming has been discussed in theory when it comes to operating systems. Formal verification is important because concurrent programs usually contain a big number of hidden bugs. Communicating sequential processes is the mathematical approach that studies communication and concurrency. Alternatively, concurrency can be modeled using machines that are finite, and such machines include Mealy and Moore, which is utilized in digital electronic systems as design tools and are encountered in the telecommunication and electronic hardware used in devices.

There are a lot of analogies between programming and computer communication. A protocol's transfer mechanism, in this case, is comparable to the central processing unit. Among the programmers, there are rules governing the design of protocols that can cooperate even when independent of each other.

We have mentioned layering before in the book, and now, we delve deeper into it. Usually, protocols are layered to form what is known as a protocol stack. As a protocol design principle, layering involves breaking protocols into smaller pieces, each of which will work to accomplish a specific task while interrelating, in trivial and undefined ways, with the other aspects of the protocol. The idea behind layering is that it allows individual aspects of the protocol to undergo testing and design without having to face combined explosion cases, and yet, the design can be kept relatively simple.

Internet communication protocols are made for complex yet diverse settings. Their design, however, is simple and modular and fit into the coarse hierarchy of function as defined within the internet protocol suite. The first cooperating protocol, the TCP/IP protocol, was a result of the decomposition of the Transmission Control Program, and what resulted was a layered communication tool. Another model is the OSI model, which consists of seven layers, as we have mentioned earlier. This one was modeled as something that would eventually guide general communication and has strict guidelines of protocol interaction, as well as rigorous notions of layering as a functionality concept.

Application software is constructed on a layer of data transport, and under the data transport layer, there is delivery of datagram and a typically connectionless routing mechanism on the internet. The relaying of packets happens in a layer that involves network link technologies such as Ethernet. Layering, hence, provides the opportunity for exchanging of technologies whenever there is a need. As such, sometimes, protocols are stacked in different arrangements, such as tunneling, that allows the connection of networks that are not similar. The asynchronous transfer mode has the internet protocol tunneled across it.

Protocol Layering

Protocol layering forms the basis for protocol design. Apart from allowing decomposition of single and complex protocols, a functional decomposition additionally exists. Each protocol goes into a protocol layer, which is essentially a functional class. The suite of internet protocol contains the network interfaces that serve as functions, including the application-transport-internet. The diagram below expresses protocol layering:

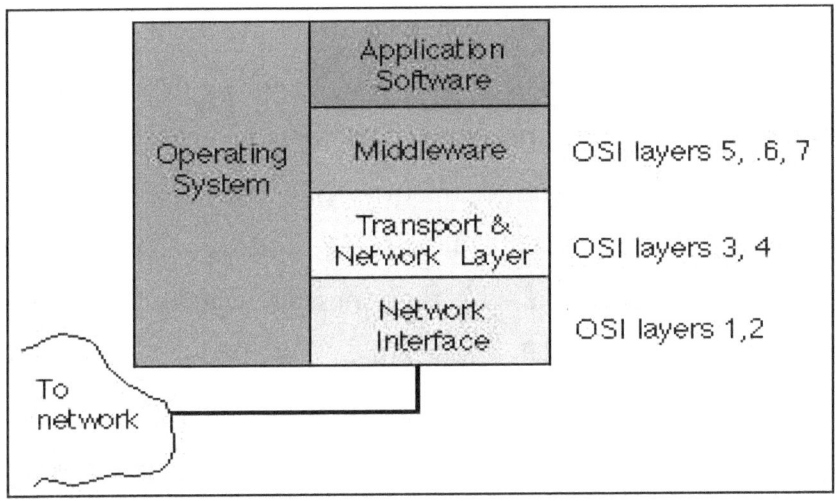

In networking, computations and algorithms go together while communication and data involve messages and protocols. A data flow diagram, therefore, consists of messages flowing. In a message flow diagram, the system has a vertical flow in protocols and a horizontal flow between systems. This flow is governed by data formats and rules as specified by protocols. Vertical protocols are, however, unlayered mainly because they are not obedient to layering principles that stipulate that protocols must be layered to enable the layer at the destination that accepts the same object handed by the source layer. Horizontal protocols, on the other hand, are layered and obey the layering principles as they are from a protocol suite. The designer of the protocol is permitted by the protocol layer to focus on a certain layer at a time or an instance, while it does have to worry about the performance of other layers.

The vertical protocols do not need to be identical in the two systems. There is a need, despite this, to satisfy even the small assumptions that the principles of protocol layering are obeyed particularly for layered protocols. How? Mostly by encapsulation. A message will be divided into small pieces, and these pieces can be called either message, packets, streams, network frames, or IP datagrams. The names will largely depend on the layer in which they are. The header area data contain information that classifies the source, as well as the packet's final destination on the network or packet. For vertical protocols, the rule is that transmission pieces are meant to be encapsulated in the lower protocols' data areas. The data is encapsulated as described on the side of the source, and the opposite takes place on the side of the destination. The rule of encapsulation, therefore, ensures that the rules of principles of layering persist in every transmission line except the lowest layer. For the purpose of ensuring that both sides are governed by a similar set of protocols, the messages carry information that identifies the protocol in their header.

The network's and protocol layering's design architecture are interrelated, and one cannot function without the next. To fully understand the features that define the relationship between network services and internet architecture, read below.

- The internet is a source of universal interconnection. All networks that interconnect physically appear as part of a single large network or the internet or internetwork, a concept we have discussed earlier.

- The internet addresses defined above consist of two main components: the net-id and hosted, which have been introduced earlier. The net-id gives an identification of the network, and host-id identifies who the host is. The internet address is an identification of the address to the network and not the individual computer. The net-id is useful for routers, as they decide where a packet should be sent.

- Independence in the network technology is achieved using the ARP, A low-level address resolution protocol. The ARP allows the mapping of internet addresses to physical addresses in a process called address resolution. The physical addresses, in this case, are, therefore, used by the network interface layer's protocols. The TCP/IP protocols, for instance, makes use of any underlying technology.

- Physical networks are connected through routers that function by forwarding packets between these interconnected networks. Routers, therefore, make it possible for one host to reach another on the physical network. The message will flow between two systems that are in communication and datagrams are passed from a router to another until the message reaches the intended recipient or destination on a network that is physically attached. To make the decision to deliver a datagram directly or whether it is to be sent to a router that is nearby, an IP routing table comes into the picture. An IP table typically consists of pairs of networkids and all paths that can be taken so that a destination is reached. These paths can either be those of direct delivery or it can be an indication that the address of another router can reach the destination quicker. There can be a special entry that specifies the default path that is used when there are not any other known paths.

- All networks are treated equally in this case, and, therefore, a point-to-point link, a LAN and WAN network are all considered as one network with no special privilege allotted to one or the other.

- Packet-switched system and service is an offering via the internet. This is preferred because it adopts well with different hardware, including the Ethernet. As a result, connectionless delivery implies that messages or streams can be divided into pieces that are separately multiplexed on the high speed interconnected machines that allow the concurrent use of connections. Every information piece, therefore, identifies the destination. Data packet delivery is sometimes unreliable, as mentioned earlier. Aside from the losses and delays, there can be duplication and delivery data packets that are out of order. This irregularity may be a result of a failure of the underlying networks. This unreliable connectionless system of delivery is defined by the IP. The IP is also responsible for the specification of the routing function as it chooses the path over which a set of data will be sent. TCP/IP protocols can also be used on connection-oriented systems. These systems build up exclusive use virtual circuits between receivers and senders. Once these virtual circuits are set up, IP datagrams are sent over the circuits as if they were data and are forwarded to IP protocol modules in a technique called tunneling. Tunneling is used on ATM networks and X.25 networks.

- The TCP defines the reliable stream transport service using connectionless packet delivery systems. The services and the application programs within the layer above are layered, and they are called application services that make use of the TCP. If a program wishes to have direct interaction with the packet delivery system, it does so using the user datagram protocol.

Software Layering

After the establishment of protocols and protocol layering, software design can follow. The software design is also layered in organization and has a relationship with protocol layering. To send a message on a system, the top module has to interact with the modules that are directly below it and hand over the message meant for encapsulation. The module will, therefore, encapsulate the message in the data area and fill the header with information regarding the protocol it implements. What follows is an interaction with the module below it, and it carries out the interaction by handing over the new information to the place deemed most appropriate. The module at the bottom interacts directly with the bottom module of the next system, so the message is sent across to the other system. The reverse happens on the receiving system so that the message that was sent on one system gets delivered ultimately in its original source to the module on top of the receiving system.

Sometimes, there are protocol errors. When this happens, the receiver will usually discard the received piece and send a message back to the original source about the condition. This is done by sending the message across and or sending it across the network if it happens at the bottom layer. The message is divided and reassembled at the point that introduced the reassembly or division.

The translation of programs us divided into subproblems:

- Compiler

- Assembler

- Link editor

- Loader

Translation software is also layered, and this allows independent designing of software layers. There is an analogy between programming languages and protocols, and the designers of the TCP/IP protocol were keen enough on this fact to ease the complexity that comes with translating programs when layering. Take the example of translating a pascal program that is compiled into an assembled into a program. The assembler program is assembled to the object code which links together with a library object code by a link editor. The product is an executable code that is loaded into physical memory. The modules that fall below the application layer are considered to be part of the operating system, and the data that passes within the modules are less expensive if compared to passing data between the transport layer and an application program. The operating system boundary is that which exists between the transport and application layers

Strict layering

Strict layering involves adhering strictly to a layered model. However, this practice is not usually the best when it comes to approaching networking as it can usually have an impact on performance. There somewhat has to be a trade-off between performance and simplicity within the network.

Using protocol is already universal today when it comes to computer networking. However, this does not mean that it is free from criticism as it has faced the same among researchers because abstracting protocol stacks may cause higher layers to copy the lower layers' functionality.

Development of Protocols

The selection of protocols precedes communication. The rules that govern the selection can be expressed by data structures and algorithms. Expressing algorithms in a portable software language enhances operating system and hardware independence. The protocol specification is wide, and even source codes can be considered as such. However, it is only source independence of the specification that provides wider interoperability.

The standards for protocols are created by obtaining the support of a standards organization, and obtaining this support also initiates the process of standardization. This process is what is commonly referred to as protocol development.

Voluntarily, the members of the standards organization agree to adhere to the work that results. Members, in this case, are often in control of large market shares that are relevant to the protocol and the standards are enforced by the government and in some cases, the law. This implementation of standards by law is important because standards are of importance in regards to the public interest. Unfortunately, in other cases, protocol standards may not be sufficient for widespread acceptance and hence, the source code may need to be disclosed and even enforced by the law.

There is a need for protocol standards, but to understand fully, the point is going to be demonstrated by what happened to IBM's bi-sync protocol (BSC). BSC is a link-level protocol that is used in the connection of two separate nodes. Originally, the design was meant for use with the multimode network, but his use only revealed the dearth of the protocol. There was no standardization, so what happened was that organizations and manufacturers alike felt the need to create other versions that were incompatible on their networks. They did this with many motives, including to discourage others from using any equipment designed by other manufacturers. Today, there are over 50 variants of the same BSC protocol. Having a standard would have prevented the eventualities.

On the inverse, some protocols can indeed gain market dominance without standardization. Such protocols are often referred to as de facto standards, and they are most common in developing niches and emerging markets. Also, they can be common in monopolized markets. These kinds of protocols usually hold the market in a generally negative grip, especially when the intention is to scare away competition. Historically, standardization can be viewed as a measure against the de facto standards. There are, however, positive exceptions to the ills brought about by de facto standards. For instance, if you take the case operating systems, such as the GNU/Linux, you find that there is no negative grasp of the market in any way. The sources are published for this operating system and are maintained in this way, and hence, they invite competition. There may be other solutions for open systems interconnection apart from standardization.

The Process of Standardization

The process of standardization is not really complex but involves a series of steps. First, it starts off with ISO commissioning of a sub-committee workgroup. The workgroup then does the work of issuing the working drafts and discussions that surround the protocol to interested parties, which may include other bodies involved in standardization. With such intense discussions, there is bound to be debate, a lot of questions and even disagreement on what the provisions of the standard should be and the needs that it can satisfy. All these conflicting views are always taken into consideration, and what they strive to achieve is a balance. After a compromise is reached, a draft proposal of what comprises the working group is made.

This draft proposal is then taken for discussion with the standard bodies for the member countries. Further, a discussion is also done within each country. There are more comments and suggestions that are collated, and eventually, national views come together and are formulated before being taken to the members of ISO who will vote for the proposal. If by any chance, a proposal is rejected, the draft has to consider every counter-proposal and objections and use the information to draft a new proposal that will be taken for the vote. Before the end of this process, there is usually a lot of feedback, compromise, and modification. The final draft that is considered reaches a status called draft international standard, and once it is standardized, it is considered an international standard.

The process that a draft proposal takes to reach international standard status can often take years for completion. The original draft created by the designer will differ significantly from the copy that makes it the standard and will have some of the features outlined below:

- Various modes of operation that will allow for different aspects of performance, for instance, the set-up of different packet sizes at the time of startup. This is usually advisable when parties are unable to reach a consensus on what should be the optimum packet size.

- Undefined parameters or some that are allowed to take values that are set at the discretion of the implementer. This, just like the various modes of operation described above, usually is a reflection of how much the views of the members conflicted.

- Parameters that are reserved for use in the future. This usually reflects that the members of the standardization board reached a consensus that the facility had to be provided. However, in such a case, they could not agree on how the facility should have been provided within the time they had available.

- There will be ambiguities and inconsistencies found as the standards continue to be implemented.

- OSI standardization

Before the internet, there was ARPANET. For the ARPANET, protocols were standardized. However, we had described above how sometimes standardization may not be enough. The reasons stated in the case of de facto standards are different from the case here. Here, what makes standardization insufficient is the fact that the protocol also needed a framework to enable operation. There is, hence, a need to develop a future-proof, framework that is also for general purposes that is suitable for protocols that are structured. Such developments are important because they would not only allow clearly definitions of the protocol responsibilities at different levels but also, they would be instrumental for prevention of overlapping functionalities. These needs resulted in the development of the OSI Open Systems Interconnection model for reference. The OSI Open Systems Interconnection reference model is a vital framework used for designing standard services and protocols that conform to the different layer specifications.

With this OSI model, the systems in communication are presumed connected through an underlying medium that provides a primary mechanism for transmission. The above layers are numbered from one through to 7, and each layer provides service to the layer above it using the services of the below layers. The interface through which the layers communicate with each other are called service access points, and the corresponding layers at the systems are known as peer entities. For communication to happen, the peer entities in a layer use a protocol that is implemented by a number layer below. If systems do not have a direct connection, relays-intermediate peer entities are used. There are addresses that identify service access points, and the domains that provide these naming services are not necessarily restricted to one layer. This makes it possible to use the same naming domain in all layers. Each layer has two protocols: the service standards protocol and the protocol standards. Service standards define how a layer communicates with the one above it while the protocol layer defines communication between peer entities at each level.

Below, there is an explanation of the layers and functionalities of the original RM/OSI model. The order is from the lowest to the highest.

1. **The physical layer.** This layer describes all the physical connections, such as electrical characteristics and the transmission techniques used. It also includes the setup, clearing, and even maintenance of the physical connections.

2. **The data link layer.** The data link layer is responsible for setting up, maintaining, and releasing data link connections. Any errors that occur in the physical layer can be detected here and, subsequently, corrected. These errors are reported to the next layer, the network layer. This layer also defines the exchange of data link units.

3. **The network layer.** The network layer is responsible for setting up, maintaining, and releasing network paths to be used between transport peer entities. The layer also provides relay and routing functions as needed, and with the transport layer, it negotiates the quality of service at the set-up of the connection. The layer also takes responsibility for controlling network congestion.

4. **The transport layer.** The transport layer provides the basis for transparent yet reliable transfer of data in a way that is cost-effective as described by the quality of service selected. This layer supports the multiplexing of many transport connections on a network. Also, it may support the split of a transport connection into many others.

5. **The session layer.** The session layer provides a variety of services to the presentation layer, including establishing and releasing session connections and quarantine services for sending presentation entities to instruct the entity receiving the session so that the latter is instructed not to release data to the presentation entity without any permission. It also establishes and releases normal and expedited exchange of data and performs interaction management so that presentation entities are able to determine whose turn it is to perform some control, resynchronize a session connection, and to report unrecoverable exceptions to the entity of presentation.

6. **Presentation layer.** The presentation layer provides services to the application layer, including the request to establish a session and to the transferring of data. Also, it allows the negotiation of which syntax is supposed to be used between the layers of application. It also

performs special-purpose transformations, for instance, data encryption and data compression.

7. **Application layer.** The application layer provides services to application processes, including identifying the intended partners of communication and establishing the necessary authority to allow communication. Also, it plays a role in determining the availability and authentication of partners and agrees on the privacy mechanisms necessary for communication and agrees on the responsibility for recovery and how to ensure data integrity and allows synchronization between application processes that cooperate. Also, it identifies any constraints, including data ad character constraints on syntax. Lastly, it also provides services dealing with cost determinations and acceptable service quality and selects dialogue discipline, such as what logon and logoff procedures are to be followed.

The table below represents the seven layers.

OSI Layer	Name	Common Protocols
7	Application	HTTP | FTP | SMTP | DNS | Telnet
6	Presentation	
5	Session	
4	Transport	TCP | SPX
3	Network	IP | IPX
2	Data Link	Ethernet
1	Physical	

The RM/OSI layering scheme defers from the TCP/IP layering scheme because it does not assume a connectionless network. The RM/OSI has a connection-oriented network, and this type is more suited for local area networks. The use of connections for communication implies that there are virtual and circuit sessions are used hence the session layer and lack of one in the TCP/IP model of layering. ISO constituent members were concerned mainly with wide area networks, and the development on the RM/OSI reflects this as it concentrates on networks with connections. Connectionless networks were mentioned as an addition to the RM/OSI. Today, however, the RM/OSI model includes connectionless services, and this has caused the TCP and IP models to develop into international standards.

Cable Infrastructure

Structured cabling is typically a type of open network structure that is usable by data, access control, telephony, and building automation systems, among others. It is a source of economical operation and flexibility

- Concepts of data rate, bandwidth, and throughput

  All network connections have what is known as data rates. A data rate is a rate at which bits are transmitted. In some networks, for instance, LANs, data varies with time. Throughput is a related concept that essentially refers to the effective rate of transmission when taking into account factors such as protocol inefficiencies, transmission overheads and competing traffic. Usually, throughput is measured at higher network layers compared to data rates. Bandwidth refers to either throughputs or data rates but is mostly used in relation to the data rate. Commonly also, the term is used in relation to radios, where bandwidth refers to the width of frequency band available and use proportional or equal to the data rate achievable.

When referring to TCP, an alternative term, 'good put,' is used to refer to the throughput of the application layer. When good put is calculated, retransmitted data can only be counted once. The measurement of data rates is done in kilobits or megabits per second (bps). When calculating data rates, remember that a kilobit is 10^3 while a megabit is 10^6.

- Concept of packets

The concept of packets is the brainchild of Paul Baran. In 1962, Baran wondered how networks would survive in the event of node failure. This kind of failure existed mainly because there were centrally switched protocols. Donald Davies in 1964 developed the same concept, giving it the name which it still uses today: packets and packet switching

Simply put, packets are modest-sized data buffers that get transmitted through shared links as a unit. Usually, packets come prefixed with a header that contains information for delivery. Just imagine how every envelope comes with a name to ensure delivery to the right place. Headers in datagram forwarding, for instance, contain a destination address while headers in networks have an identifier for the virtual circuit; most networking today is based on the use of packets. Packets are called frames when they are in the LAN layer and segments when in the transport layer. LANs have an intrinsic maximum packet size that they can support and usually, this comes to around 1500 bytes of data for Ethernet. TCP originally held 512 bytes. You may wonder how packets are transferred from large data pockets to smaller ones, but this shall be addressed later on in the book.

Every layer adds its header: typically, IP headers-20 bytes, Ethernet headers-14 bytes, and TCP headers-20 bytes, and IP headers-20 bytes. Datagram forwarding networks have headers that contain the delivery information, including destination address. Internal network nodes are called switches/routers, and these will ensure that the packet is delivered to the specified address.

- Concept of datagram forwarding

When a packet has to be delivered, there is a data packet that contains a destination address. The switches and routers on the way must observe the address and deliver the packet to the destination. The packet can only be delivered to the right destination by the provision of each router with a forwarding table of pairs. This is typically the destination, next, hop pair. What happens is that a packet arrives then the switch/router will look up the next destination address in the forwarding table. When this information is looked up, then it is easy to find the next_hop information. The next_hop information is the immediate next address in the loop that the packet should be forwarded to so that it is one more step closer to its destination. Every router or switch is responsible for only one step in the path that is meant to deliver the packet to its destination. When all is well within the layer, a packet is delivered to its destination, one hop at a time without interference.

The destination entries are in a forwarding table. However, they do not necessarily usually correspond with the destination addresses except in the forwarding of Ethernet datagrams. What happens with IP routing is that the destination entries in the table will often correspond to the prefixes of the IP address. This is a strategy that is meant for saving space. The requirement here is that switches can perform lookup operations using the destination address and forwarding table in the packet that has just arrived to determine what the next hop should be.

LANs and Ethernet

Below is a simple diagram that captures the components of a local area network.

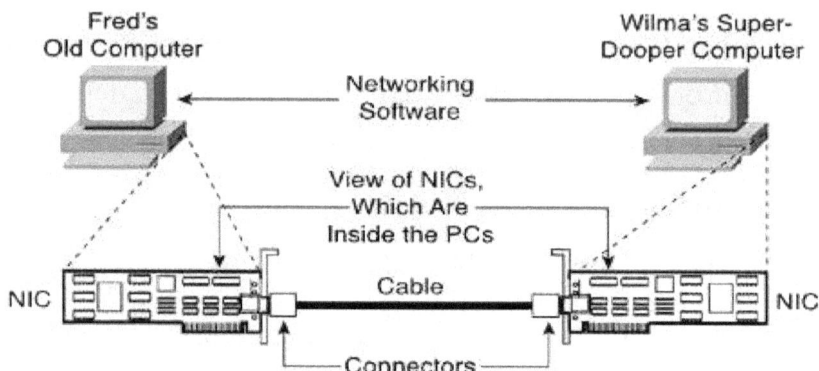

As earlier defined, LAN stands for local area networks. A LAN consists of physical links (serial lines), interfacing software that is common and connecting the hosts to the links and protocols that link everything together.

Ethernet is a physical/data link layer. As a physical layer of the network, Ethernet focuses on hardware elements, for instance, cables, network interface cards, and repeaters. Ethernet is the most used protocol in the physical layer. For instance, the Ethernet network specifies the type of cables that can be used, the topology and the length of cables.

The data link layer addresses how data packets are sent from node to node, and Ethernet makes use of the CSMA/CD access. SCMA/CD stands for carrier sense multiple access/collision detection. The SCMA/CD is a system in which a computer must put an ear out for the cable before sending information through the network. If there is a clear way, then the computer will continue with the transmission. If there is another node that is already doing the transmission, then the computer will have to wait before trying to transmit again once the line is clear. In other instances, two computers may want to transmit at the same time, and this causes what is known as a collision. In such a case, the computers will both take a step back and try to transmit again after random amounts of time before trying to retransmit. It is common for collisions to happen with this type of access method. This type of delay is, however, not big and usually small and does not affect transmission speeds on the network.

Originally, Ethernet was developed in 1983 and had speeds of 10Mbps. While this may not look like much now, it was good speed in the early days. Ethernet used a coaxial cable. The Ethernet protocol allows bus, star, and tree topologies, and these may depend on the type of cables used. The original Ethernet cabling was heavy and expensive to purchase and even install. Maintenance was an issue, and there was no easy way to retrofit the coaxial cable into existing facilities. The current Ethernet cables are now modified and use a twisted pair wire. They can transmit at speeds of 10, 00 and 1000 megabits per second.

The fast Ethernet protocol transmits at speeds of up to 100 Mbps and requires the use of not only different but also expensive network hubs and interface cards. Also, they make use of 5 twisted pair of optic fiber. There is also Gigabit Ethernet that has transmission speeds of 1Gbps, which is the same as 1000 Mbps. It is used along copper and fiber optic cabling. A summary of an Ethernet protocol is shown below:

Protocol	Cable	Speed
Ethernet	Twisted Pair, Coaxial, Fiber	10 Mbps
Fast Ethernet	Twisted Pair, Fiber	100 Mbps
Gigabit Ethernet	Twisted Pair, Fiber	1000 Mbps

Chapter 7: Servers and Virtualization

Imagine a typical data enterprise center with many servers. The majority of these servers sit idle as the workload of the enterprise is distributed among a small number of servers. This results in what can be considered a waste of resources, as these systems are not at work and yet will use power, require maintenance, and even cooling. This is a problem in many work environments today, and this is the exact kind of situation that server virtualization intends to solve. In this chapter, an exploration of server virtualization is done. The concept is explained, and so is the benefit of the approach.

Components of a Server

A server, basically, is also a type of computer. However, depending on the type of server in question, they are always set up differently from the average personal computer used by the average consumer. All the different kinds of hosting all involve the use of dedicated servers. However, the difference between shared, cloud, and VPS hosting are that the servers are organized and structured differently. The key components of a server are outlined below.

There are different components in servers; some are basic, while others are optional. They include the following.

Motherboard

The most basic explanation of a motherboard is that it is a circuit board that ensures the connection of all server components. This is where the heartbeat of the server is, and most consumers know little to nothing about it. The most important point to note when it comes to the motherboard is that it dictates the type of CPU, number of hard drives, and the amount of RAM that is needed for connection to the server.

Central Processing Unit

This component is also known as the processor, and it works like the brain of the server. It regulates performance but is not the only component that matters when it comes to performance. However, the importance of the CPU is trivialized. It is important for even the average consumer to understand the importance of processors and what makes a good CPU. You need to get enough information so that you know if you are getting a good deal on a central processing unit. Different hosts may offer outdated models or consumer-grade processors instead of the current gen-server grade processors.

Random Access Memory

Servers cannot be complete without memory, especially if the hosting of websites is involved. In the server, memory refers to the RAM and not the hard drive. RAM is similar to the human brain's short-term and is critical for the server's performance and the amount of memory that will need to be scaled up to meet the needs of the host. Apart from quantities, quality should also be considered when talking about RAM. There are four RAM generations currently, and the newer versions run faster than the older ones. To ensure that you have the best, look for the latest RAM technology as this will result in the highest value for your money and the best performance.

Network Connection

The network connection is yet another important component of servers. Servers are often connected to ports whose speeds are set by the host and can vary. Most of them start at 10Gbps, and others can go as high as Gigabit connections.

Hard Drive

The hard drive is yet another component of a server. The ultimate hard drive today is the SATA drive as they offer reliability and stellar performance. However, as is the case with many technological inventions, there are already better inventions threatening to take the place of SATA drives, for instance, Solid State Drives. All servers are beginning to embrace SSDs because they offer superior speeds for reading and writing, and they are highly reliable. Getting an SSD means a move towards increased server performance.

Graphics Processing Unit (An Optional Component)

Traditionally, GPUs were used only for gaming and graphic interfaces. Over time, however, these components have found their way in servers. They are accessed through a command line or terminal. There are other high-end GPUs that today are used in place of CPUs. Most servers, however, do not consist of GPUs. The ones that will be putting them in place are those that deal with artificial intelligence and machine learning especially

What Is Server Virtualization?

Server virtualization is a process through which software on a physical server is aided to create a number of virtual instances that can run independently. On a dedicated server, the machine has one operating system. However, with a virtual server, one machine can be able to run multiple instances, all of which will have independent operating systems. In this process, a physical server is taken, and the virtualization software helps to partition it and divide it so that it created what was referred to above as virtual instances. The entire system is dedicated to one thing, and thus, the server can be used in many different ways. So, unlike in the past before virtualization was mainstream, an operating system does not require a physical platform to host an operating system. A hypervisor is used to share the hardware of the host with the individual virtual machines. This technique, therefore, allows the sharing of resources, which enables organizations to reduce the cost of running a lot of physical software and reduce their datacenter hardware footprints.

Another way through which the concept of server virtualization can be understood is through the host/guest paradigm. Every gust will run on a virtual imitation of what would be considered the hardware layer. The guest OS runs without modifications and also allows the administrator to play the role of creating guests that use a different OS. The guest, in this case, does not usually know anything about the operating system of the host

The concept of data virtualization only hit the waves recently, and yet it has been in the oven for well over 50 years. IBM was the pioneer organization when it came to virtualization of system memory. This would eventually act as the precursor to virtualization hardware. IBM created the VM/370, a propriety operating system. This operating system level of virtualization does not have much significance beyond mainframe computing, but even through its simplicity, it developed to the z/VM, which was the first virtual platform for severs that was used for commercial purposes in the market.

Today, server virtualization has become a norm, and the concept became dominant in the IT industry. Several companies are moving towards full virtualization and cloud-managed information technology ecosystems. This trend of virtualization's popularity came to life in the 90s with the release of the VMware workstation by VMware. The VMWare workstation was a savior that enabled the virtualization of x86/x64 machines and architecture and popularized virtualization. It became possible to run Windows, MacOS, and Linux on one host hardware, and, therefore, over the past two decades, virtualization of servers has served an important role in shaping the IT infrastructure market.

For virtualized server platforms, it is necessary to have a vendor or host hardware available. The hardware, in most cases, is usually a server that requires software as described above. The software is called hypervisor. The role of the hypervisor is to present the generic virtualized hardware to the operating systems that are installed onto it. The hardware included all the components needed to start the operating system, including the CPU, network drivers, hard disks, SCSI drivers, and memory allocations. The hypervisor, therefore, manages the resources of the host and allocates the same resources to every virtual machine that depends on it.

Virtualization can happen in either Windows, Linux, and Aix operating systems. Even more interesting is the fact that manufacturers are now offering virtual appliances of hardware devices. For example, Network Load balancers were traditionally physical devices in a rack. Today, however, things have changed, and they are many times virtualized. There is more power in host hardware, so offering virtualized dedicated appliances is quickly becoming commonplace.

There are several types of hypervisors. Below, we discuss information about hypervisors in detail.

As you may have already gathered, the hypervisor is the primary software that is meant to enable virtualization in servers. There are mainly two types of hypervisors:

- Baremetal. This is what is commonly referred to as the Type 1 hypervisor and is often installed directly on the host hardware. Directly, this hypervisor manages all the resources of server hardware that are installed in the bare-metal tin. Every hardware resource in this hardware is then allocated to virtual machines through the Hypervisor Operating system.

- The Type 2 Hypervisor. This hypervisor runs directly on top of the conventional operating system. It does so as an application or process. It virtualizes the hardware resources found in the conventional operating system. Interestingly, this type of hypervisor is common in non-production environments, and an example is the VMWare Workstation and Virtual Box.

Today, the VMware company has managed to keep every other manufacturer busy such that it has dominated the virtualization industry. So the software has ended up in use in many of the world's data centers. A giant in IT, Microsoft, produced its own version of the hypervisor-Hyper-V back in 2008. This hypervisor comes up with almost all Microsoft server operating systems, but recently, there has been a newer addition as the package comes bundled with Windows 10 Professional. The open-source community has its own hypervisor, known as Xen. Xen is a creation of the Cambridge University during the 1990s. However, it has continued to play a vital role in the world of virtualization today. It is, for instance, Amazon's virtual platform for cloud-based Amazon Web Services. Since Amazon is winning in the cloud ecosystem, other companies use Xen as a commercial product.

Server virtualization is not just a thing for software manufacturers. In fact, today, IBM, a company that manufactures its own hardware is a major manufacturer of hypervisors. The platforms of IBM, including System I, System Z, and System P, use the para-virtual hypervisor. The guest virtual machines have prior knowledge of each other and the resource requirements allotted to them through their host. The hardware resources of the host are divided and allocated to the virtual machine. Through this sharing, every partition knows of the partition requirements of the other, and every server has the least minimum hardware designed.

There is also operating system virtualization. At this level, virtualization works differently. There is no basis on the host/guest paradigm. Instead, the host runs an operating system kernel as the core and distributes the functionalities of the operating system to the guests. Guests then use the same operating system as the host, but it is allowed to use different distributions of the same system. Distributing architecture like this eliminates the system calls between layers, thus reducing the overhead of CPU usage. Each partition also remains isolated strictly from a neighbor so that security breaches and failure in a partition does not affect other partitions. Common libraries and binaries are shared on the same physical machine, which allows the operating system level virtual server to host an infinite number of guests all at once.

Server virtualization is part of an overall trend toward virtualization in IT involving enterprises. It works alongside network virtualization, storage virtualization, and management of workloads. Server virtualization is a component in autonomic computing development, which aims to enable the server to manage itself based on the perceived activity.

Types of server virtualization

There is more than one way through which virtualization can be achieved, apart from para virtualization that has been discussed. The ones that will be discussed below are:

- OS level virtualization

- Para virtualization

- Full virtualization

These share a few common traits, for example, they all have a physical server that is referred to as the host, and the virtual servers are called guests. The virtual servers exhibit behavior similar to physical machines, and every system uses a different approach for the allocation of physical server resources for virtual server needs.

Full virtualization. Full virtualization makes use of the hypervisor software. This hypervisor directly interacts with the CPU's and disk space's physical servers. The hypervisor serves as a platform that can be used by the operating systems of the virtual servers. The hypervisor does the work of keeping every virtual server independent and even unaware of the other virtual servers that are running on the same machine. Every guest server runs an operating system, and they do not have to be the same. One could be utilizing a Windows operating system, while the other operates a Linux operating system. The hypervisor also monitors the resources of the physical server. The hypervisor relays resources to the appropriate virtual server from the physical machine. The virtual servers, at this time, are running application. The hypervisor, as an application, has its own processing needs, and as such, the physical server reserves some processing resources and power that ensure the running of the hypervisor. If there are no reserve resources, then the overall performance of the system can be affected, and the speeds become slower.

Para virtualization. As a concept, para virtualization is a different approach from the full version. In para virtualization, the guest servers are aware of the existence of each other. The hypervisor in this type of virtualization does not do the kind of processing power needed to operate a guest operating system like in the full virtualization model. This is because there are interaction and recognition of the operating systems that are within the server without discrimination of one of them. There is a cohesive way of working here where the system is involved.

Operating system virtualization. This type of virtualization does not use a hypervisor in any way. The capability to virtualize is already part of the operating system. The operating system, in this case, performs the functions of a virtualized hypervisor. There is, however, a limitation to this approach. Every virtual server in this setup remains independent of the guest servers within the network, and there is no way that is operating among different operating systems. The environments in which the guest OS operates should be similar. As such, this type of environment is called a homogenous environment.

There is really no type of virtualization that is better over another. The choice to use usually depends largely on the needs of the network administrator. If the physical servers of the administrator run on the same operating system, then the operating system type of virtualization may be appropriate as these systems will be efficient and faster compared to further approaches. If alternatively, the administrator runs different servers on a variety of OS, then the network administrator may resort to the use of para virtualization. However, there is one disadvantage that may come with using para-virtualization, which is lack of support. Compared to the other types, this is a relatively new type of technique, and, therefore, only some organizations offer materials for para virtualization. Many organizations mainly back the use of para virtualization. However, para virtualization is quickly taking over and may eventually replace full virtualization.

Benefits of Server Virtualization

There are benefits to using server virtualization, and it is no wonder that many organizations invest in it. There are reasons that address technicalities, while others are purely based on financial motivations. Below, we outline the benefits of using server virtualization

- Through the method of consolidation virtualization helps in conserving space. Each server is dedicated to one solicitation. However, should many applications only make use of a minor quantity of electricity for processing, it is possible for the administrator of the system to combine many computers into one server that can run in different virtual environments. This can especially be helpful and beneficial for companies that have multiple servers, as it will significantly reduce or eliminate the need for servers.

- This technique provides a loophole through which companies can tend to like termination, all minus buying more components. Redundancy is when only one app is run on different servers. Often, it is practiced as a way to ensure safety such that if one server does not work well for whatever cases, then the other that is running this place can conveniently be a replacement. Through redundancy, there is a reduction in the service. It is not sensible to construct two servers (virtual) that perform the same presentation on a real server. In such a case, a crash in the server would mean that two virtual servers also fail. For many cases, people working within the system have the tendency to make redundant virtual servers on real technologies.

- Virtual servers give structures that are not only independent but also isolated so that programmers are able to test new operating systems and applications. Instead of buying physical machines, a virtual server can simply be created on the existing machine by the network administrator. Virtual servers are usually independent of the other servers, which give the programmer an opportunity to run the software as they need without worrying about the effect it will have on other applications.

- Server hardware eventually ends up obsolete. This creates further problems because, usually, switching across two differing systems proves to be not easy. Systems such as these can be referred to as legacy systems and offering services provided by these. These outdated systems could be the answer needed for proper functionality. In such cases, the obvious and most practical thing the system administrator can do is to create a virtual account of the hardware on a server that fits today's context. When looking at this approach like it is from the application, everything remains the same at the very core. The tasks will work the same way they would if they were still on the preliminary hardware. The company can, therefore, buy time for transitioning to new processes without having to worry about the server breaking down. This can especially be beneficial in cases where the corporation that fashioned the original hardware ceased to be, and so, it may be impossible to fix broken equipment.

- Also, migration is a trend that has come with virtualization and is, by extension, the advantage or benefit of using virtualization. If you have the right software and hardware, then it can be possible to physically remove the network of a physical machine from one to the additional. Formerly, this stood probable but merely if the two bodily technologies run on the same computer technologies that are needed, in this case, to ensure proper functionality. Today, it is possible to rove virtual servers across many different machines, even when the machines are processed rather differently due to differences in hardware. The only condition that remains is that the processors must come from the same manufacturers.

- These servers help in cost minimization within enterprises. This reduction happens because virtualization helps to increase the utilization of already existing resources, and it is an efficient solution for small to medium-scale applications. As a technology, virtualization is used as a cost-effective way of providing web hosting services. Companies will acquire much less hardware for new infrastructure, and older hardware can simply be migrated to new and more efficient hardware. This equally benefits the data centers, as there will be less power and cooling requirements and reduces the datacenter footprint, thus reducing the overall costs associated with managed service provision.

- Yet another benefit associated with virtualization is functionality. The key functions include the ability to roll back changes, which eliminates the need for the many requirements that were associated with rebuilding a network from scratch. Management features such as

Cloning, vMotion, and Fault Tolerance changed how administrators could increase infrastructure uptime while offering the best service level agreement to customers. As a result, network administrators can deploy new virtual machines almost instantly through the use of templates. Server provisioning has equally improved. Now, it is possible to build new virtual infrastructure from scripts. With tools such as Terraform, you can build virtual networks and use other toolsets for configuration such as Ansible to configure new infrastructure in exact and uniform ways as per the requirements.

- Lastly, virtualization has played a vital role in improving disaster recovery. You do not need to restore lost data from a tap to re-provisioned hardware as would have been the case in the past. Instead, you can replicate the entire virtual network infrastructure between sites using different tools that are required for virtualization. These tools may include VMware Site Recovery Manager, which can be automated. Other products, for example, CloudEndure can replicate servers to the cloud, and the entire system is replicated in a staging area that can be activated when a disaster recovery scenario is invoked.

Limitations of Server Virtualization

Above, we have explored the different benefits of server virtualization. But just like every other thing, server virtualization also has its limitations. It is vital for a network administrator to investigate the changing of servers and their architecture so that they can engineer the right solution.

One of the limitations is that if you have servers that are dedicated to applications that have high demands on power for processing, then this may not be the most viable choice. Virtualization works by dividing the processing power of the server among the virtual ones. When the processing power of the server is unable to meet the demand of the application, then the entire system will slow down. Even tasks that typically take a short time for completion begin to take hours. There is also a possibility of the system crashing if the server cannot meet the demands of all the virtual servers within the system. As such, it is vital that the network administrator takes a close look at the use of the CPU before the physical server is divided into several virtual machines.

Additionally, there is a limitation in migration. It is possible to carry out a migration of a virtual server from a physical device to the next if, together, the equipment makes use of a unified constructor's design. When a system customs a single server, that, for instance, goes on an AMD workstation, and an added one customs an Intel processor, it will be intolerable to carry out porting in a virtual server from a physical machine to the next. You may wonder why an administrator would require the migration of a virtual server from a physical machine. The physical server may require maintenance and porting the simulated ones to supplementary equipment can help in reducing the downtime of the app. Relocation is, hence, important because when migration ceases to be a preference, the requests that run on the computer-generated server will be unavailable until maintenance is done.

The downsides of virtualization are not as many as the benefits, and with the right considerations in place, a network administrator can identify the type that will work efficiently for the enterprise. The benefits are the reason that many companies are still investing in the virtualization of servers. Technology keeps advancing, and as this happens, the need for big data centers continues to decrease as well. The power consumption of servers may also be on the way, and this makes the concept of virtualization not only attractive financially but also a green alternative that can help in the reduction of the carbon blueprint of many companies. As networks use servers, there will be the development of more efficient yet larger computer networks. In fact, virtual servers can top an upheaval in the computing trade over time.

Determining if Server Virtualization Is Necessary for Your Business

If you are wondering if server virtualization is what may be best for your company and you need a few pointers to help you start, then the following section may be useful to you.

Server virtualization brings together multiple operating systems on one server. You can consider it if you need any of the things described below:

- If you need to use more operating systems and applications without necessarily breaking the budget for electricity, space, and hardware, then virtualization may be the best option for you. This is because the approach can be instrumental in reducing all these while not affecting the enterprise's budget in the long-term.

- Also, if you wish to reduce the work hours for your IT staff so that they do not have to spend a lot of time on patching, installation, administration and supporting application servers, then this may be the right time for you as it is an approach that consolidates many of these aspects, making work easier.

- If you wish or need to simplify backup and reduce the downtimes of applications, by adding storage space, then virtualization is the best option for you and should ultimately be considered.

- Sometimes, you may need to expand your technical skills in the field of networking. Server virtualization may help you to learn the ins and outs of converging network operations and systems. In such cases, virtualization would be the right step to take.

- Virtualization may also be the best option for you if you feel that you need to master cloud challenges. With experience in handling cloud challenges, you will be better placed when your business will be migrating to virtualization. This is especially critical when you will eventually have to migrate services that are critical to your business to the cloud.

Just like with other technologies, virtualization involves more than just the purchase and installation of a product. There are four important steps that can be considered part of the virtualization process:

1. Evaluation of the network's and system's current capacity and performance and the requirements it may need in the future

   When you consider the above, you may find that you are long overdue for a refresh at your enterprise. You know that it is time for a haul in your systems when you experience server sprawl, and you struggle to achieve stellar performance with old hardware. When looking at the systems, consider the capacity and speeds of the central processing unit, a disk I/O, and processors. You can also have a look at emails, servers, setup of the hard disk, database applications, and file servers when evaluating where virtualization could lead to improvement. At network levels, you should assess the performance of routing, switching, and even WAN links. Acceleration of the wide-area network, for example, can make such a big difference in performance.

2. Calculation of the expected payoff if the system or network is virtualized

Look at your enterprise or business and try to establish what you will gain from embracing virtualization. Consider the enterprise's short and long-term goals and establish how they fit in with the possibility of virtualization. Consider when you should do it and make further evaluations so that you do not find yourself on the losing end when it comes to virtualization. Look at what you can use in your new endeavor and establish if indeed, it is the right choice for you.

3. Creation of a strong infrastructure

You can choose a virtualization technology at this point, but you have to ensure that this will be a technology that will work to improve performance while simultaneously reducing costs and complexity at the moment and in the future, too. You could look for a management interface that provides a single interface for the management of the infrastructure and ensures performance and reduction in costs. Consider what switches you will use, hypervisors, storage, and servers.

4. Map your timeline for virtualization

   By the time you will be reaching this stage, you will have all the software and hardware that will be needed for virtualization. The timeline for migration can range from anywhere in a time frame of as little as two weeks, and sometimes, it can go for as long as three months. The time frame will depend on the number of servers and sites and the staff.

From the start, align the network staff and the servers of the company so that you do not end up with high operating costs. The person who deals with the systems will need expertise and skills in managing operating systems, applications, switching, traffic, and VLAN. The network person should understand how to do things such as pushing the quality of service in servers. This is really important because the performance of your network may depend on these people. If it is impossible to have people who can manage these tasks, then you will have to bring in expertise from the outside. With the right tools and virtualization expertise, you can plan and take the virtualization journey that will best fit your organization.

The Potential in Server Virtualization and the Trend It Is Likely to Take

After all is said and done, you may be wondering why it is important to learn about server virtualization. Below, I explain why it is important to learn about server virtualization if you have even the slightest interest in networking.

Virtualization of servers is a simple concept that has had a profound and even almost profound impact on data centers in many enterprises. It had its roots in the early 60s and was popularized by VMware. The virtualization software was later introduced in the early 2000s for the x86 servers. Since the inception of these servers, many other vendors have begun to develop their own platforms for server-virtualization, and there have been advancements in management, automation, and orchestration. These tools make it easy to deploy, move, and manage virtual machine networks with ease. Before virtualization, many enterprises had to deal with server sprawl, high energy bills, and underutilized computer power, all to be dealt using manual processes and with inefficiency and inflexibility in the data centers. Today, this has changed, and instead, it has become difficult to find enterprises that do not run their workloads in virtual machine environments.

However, every good thing usually meets yet another good thing that will knock it off its pedestal. The next big thing when it comes to virtualization is going small. The next way that this will transform is that developers will slice applications into microservices that are not only small but also run in containers. There shall also be experimentation with function as a service, otherwise known as server less computing.

Understanding Containers and Virtual Machines

Docker is a popular tool used for spinning containers. Kubernetes is an innovation of Google. These two are the major enablers for containerization as they help in the management of multiple containers. Containers can be thought of as execution environments that share the host operating system's kernel. They are self-contained, streamlined and even more lightweight compared to virtual machines as they bypass any startup overhead and redundant guest operating systems. Developers are, therefore, able to run as many as approximately 6 to 8 more times of containers as virtual machines on one hardware.

So far, containers seem to be a good thing. However, they also have a downside. The use of containers is a relatively new approach, and therefore, there is not a wealth of management tools that are associated with older technologies. There is, therefore, still a lot of work-related to set-up and maintenance that is yet to be done. Additionally, as a new technology, there are also concerns about the security of the containers.

Where virtual machines are concerned, it is relatively easy to move workloads from one host to another. However, bare-metal machines complicate such a movement because they make it hard to move or upgrade. This difficulty comes about because rolling back a machine on a machine state with bare metal servers can be challenging.

Server less Computing and Virtual Machines

In the traditional cloud movement, there is the provisioning of virtual machines, databases, storage, and every other associated management and security tools. After this, applications are loaded on to the virtual machine.

Server less computing, on the other hand, is different. In this case, the developers will write the code, and the other aspects are handled by cloud service providers. Developers do not have to contemplate operating systems, servers, managing, and provisioning. Even the physical server that runs the code is the responsibility of the cloud service provider. The code is broken down into specific functions instead of having a monolithic application. When an event occurs and triggers a function, the server less service runs the function. Customers are charged by function as specified by server less providers. With the container and microservices, server less computing usually bypasses virtual machine layers, and the functions run on bare metal. Server less computing is currently immature, and the cases where they are used are limited.

The use of containers is increasing, and server less computing as a concept is also growing. Server virtualization is a solid technology that will continue to power many applications in the enterprise environment. The saturation of virtual machines in the enterprise world is estimated to be as high as 90 %.

It is currently hard to think that enterprises can move their critical applications that run smoothly to either server less platforms or containers. More likely is the probability of having heterogeneous environments in which the use of virtual machines will still be common. Containers still need to run on the same operating system and cannot be mixed between Windows and Linux.

There are new applications that rebuilt with the latest agile methodologies and DevOps because developers now have an easier time with all the options available. They will be able to make case-by-case decisions whether they should run a new workload in either a container, virtual machine, or server less environment.

Chapter 8: Securing Computer Networks

As discussed in the earlier chapters, network security is a term that refers to the extensive policies, as well as procedures that an administrator implements in order to evade and keep track of various unauthorized access, modification, denial, and exploitation of the existing network and its resources. This implies that a properly implemented network security system is capable of blocking hackers and viruses from gaining access to secure information or altering it therein. There are different layers of network security systems. The first one is usually enforced by using a username mechanism that allows specifically authorized persons who have a tailored privilege. When the user is authenticated, accessibility becomes easier. But, even in this case, firewalls won't always be in a position to easily detect, as well as stop viruses from penetrating the network security platform. In that case, the malware can contribute to the loss of crucial information. Therefore, antivirus software and intrusion prevention system will be implemented in order to help prevent harmful malware from penetrating the network. In different instances, network security has been confused with the use of information security systems. This has a different unique scope that intensely interrelates to the integrity of data of various forms, including print, as well as electronic.

With that said, network security systems combine a broad range of several layers aimed at creating a defense mechanism on the network. Every network layer works by implementing various policies and controls. Therefore, users are authorized to gain access to various resources of networks. Malicious actors will be blocked from accessing the said network or rather threatening the network system and security. When used properly, network security systems help the user, in most cases, organizations to prevent thieves from penetrating into their systems. This is also a move towards securing vital information embedded in the network security systems. With that said, it becomes vital to use network security systems in protecting proprietary information. In the current era, computers, as well as security breaches, are in the news every other day. They also cost many organizations millions of dollars appended to creating a security system that can help in protecting their systems. In a report by the IBM department, about 10 % of organizations in the US were subjected to computer network breach in 2018. Most companies lost sensitive information in the process. The healthcare sector has also registered vulnerable experiences and lost up to $ 300 in seeking to recover patient personal data. These facts surrounding the cybersecurity system are downright scary. With that said, it's vital to protect your system from such situations. While it can be challenging to actually find the viable means of protecting information from theft, there are a few measures that can assist you in achieving this in the long run.

The Basics of Network Security

There are different phases of implementation when it comes to network security. Network security consists of the elements outlined below:

- Protection. This involves the configuration of networks and systems as correctly as possible.

- Detection. This involves the identification of when there has been a change in the configuration or when there is a problem in the network traffic.

- Reaction. This happens after the identification of the problem. The response or reaction must be swift so that the network or system is returned to the original state as soon as possible.

Network security experts do not depend on one line of defense, as this can prove to be dangerous. A single line of defense can easily be attacked and overcome by an adversary, and yet, the network is more than just a line of defense and more of a territory. Hence, even when a part of the network has been invaded, there is a probability that they can be expelled if the network or system's defense is well-organized.

Types of Network Security

- **Control of access**. This involves preventing just any user from having access to the network. Therefore, every user and device in the network must be recognized. There are security policies imposed at this point, and they may include giving limited access or blocking noncompliant endpoint devices.

- **Antimalware and antivirus software use**. Malware includes, but is not limited, to worms, viruses, spyware, ransomware, and Trojans. Interestingly, malware can penetrate the systems of a network and remain dormant for weeks on end before attacking. It is, hence, important that a network uses anti-malware programs that will scan for malware before it enters the system and continuously track files so that it can detect and eliminate any anomalies.

- **Application security**. Applying application security means that you will protect all the software that runs your business. Some applications will have vulnerabilities and cracks through which attackers can infiltrate the network. Securing your applications will, therefore, mean protecting the hardware, software, and even processes in ways that will close all the holes available that can be exploited by hackers.

- **Behavioral analytics**. Behavioral analytics involves checking the behaviors of the network for any behavior outside the norm. For you to understand what abnormal behavior is, you must understand what normal behavior is within the network. In an enterprise or organization, the security team will usually play a critical role in helping the network identify what seems to be out of place behaviorally. They also know how to look at all the factors necessary to determine if there are indicators of the network being compromised. After identifying that, indeed, there is a threat, they can offer remedies that will help return the network back to normal.

- **Prevention of data loss**. It is beyond vital that an organization takes the right measures to ensure that their staff members do not end up sending what may be considered sensitive information outside the network as this could lead to a significant loss of data. To help with this concern, data loss prevention technologies can be put in place. These technologies will work by stopping members of staff from forwarding, uploading, or printing any information that may be considered critical for the company and if there is a general suspicion that it is being downloaded in a manner that is unsafe.

- **Email security.** In many organizations, emails are the first avenue that is used for a data breach. Social engineering tactics and personal information are common avenues through which hackers build complex phishing campaigns that are meant to cheat unsuspecting individuals and send them to sites that serve malware to their systems. Email security applications may help to enhance the security of networks in such a case by blocking any incoming attacks and controlling outbound messages that may cause a loss in the data.

- **Firewalls.** This is, perhaps, the most well-known way of enhancing security in a computer network. This happens when you put a barrier between your network, which usually is trusted and other networks such as the internet. There are both software and hardware-software, and some are a hybrid.

- **Intrusion prevention systems.** These types of networks scan network traffic so that any active attacks are blocked. Most do this by correlating the world's global threat intelligence to block malicious activities and prevent further progression of any files that they may find suspicious. This helps prevent any further malware from infiltrating the system and also prevents the spread of malware outbreaks and reinfection with the same.

Here are top strategies to use in protecting your network security system.

✓ Install a Firewall and Protective Barrier for Security

A firewall refers to a network security device that can be used in monitoring incoming, as well as outgoing traffic within the network system. It also permits or blocks any form of information such as data packets founded on a set of various security alerts and rules. In the long run, the purpose of this network security system is to create a significant barrier between the internal network and the incoming traffic that comes from external sources, including the internet. The main purpose of this interface is to block any form of intrusion from different sources. Firewalls also carefully analyze the incoming traffic. This is highly based on the pre-established rules that govern the filtering of traffic generated from different suspicious sources in order to prevent attacks. At every point of your network security, firewalls will guard traffic via the entry point known as the port. This is where the entire information is exchanged with the existing external devices. For instance, if you have an IP address in the house and a port number in the room, then you'll need to have different filters for various data provisions and dockets. The owner of the room will be allowed to gain access to specific rooms, but this is highly reliant on the authority they have in the organization. Also, children will be allowed to gain access to certain entry points within the ports.

✓ Use Virus Protection Software to Secure Your Network

Antivirus software for protection is successfully used in setting a broad spectrum of programs created to safeguard a system from malicious programs, such as malware and Trojans. Therefore, the virus protection is carefully installed into the computer system in order to protect personal property while removing any form of glitches, as well as software viruses that could be bogging down the operating system and network. With that said, there are various forms of viruses that could be bringing down your network. That is why there are multiple types of antivirus software in the industry. As such, free antivirus software offers simple scans on the computer using signature-founded detection to locate the identified malware. Other than that, pain antivirus software includes different heuristics that can be used in catching any form of imminent threats within the computer system. That implies that the antivirus can be used in creating generic signatures that can easily be used in identifying malicious intent on the internet. Virus protection software can also ensure that there's the protection of a computer's identity and data, as well as classified identification and information. In the long run, you will be allowed to optimize the company's performance, as well as security details using antivirus protection. Most individuals are pretty familiar with an element known as Trojan. However, they are not aware that it refers to a precarious element that can harm the computer system. By applying genetic systems, virus protection helps in ensuring that company performance is successfully enhanced. In other words, Trojans can easily be identified in the presence of an antivirus security system. You shall also learn more about its ability to spread via social engineering since it may be challenging to detect because it resembles the actual software that's used in computer protection. With that in mind, it's evident that clicking on a certain link or email attachment from a trusted source that could be assumed in one way or another could lead to the penetration of strange Trojan devices within the computer devices.

✓ Use a Customized VPN

While you can have a new device, apps, coupled with games, you also need to understand how to make good use of them. With professional help from a reliable service provider who understands the value of protecting your network, you can learn more about the applications of different operating systems, such as Windows,

Chrome, and macOS. You will also grasp lessons based on the vital applications of simple instructions regarding how you can install security measures into your gadget. Other than that, you will understand why it's vital to have a VPN installed on your system to enhance security. With that said, the strategy was implemented in the tech sector by some of the world's most trusted tech gurus in order to help in enhancing privacy and security. Today, most business professionals can rely on the applications of a VPN in enhancing a viable platform of security in many ways. As such, these individuals have learned the basics of incorporating a VPS into their service portfolio where the device, in this case, a gadget that has password security measures, can be used in the application of top-notch security in a certain computer system. With a VPN, you'll be able to control who can gain access into your computer by analyzing the benefits of using a VPN. As such, it has been discussed that by using this device, you will be adding another layer of security into your system. For vital instructions on how to have it installed into your gadget, you can read the manual provided by the manufacturer and take advantage of the possible hidden features presented. Also, it's vital to understand that, with a VPN, you shall be in a position to secure your WI-FI network, especially when you want to evade the invasion of prying eyes. It can also work for you if you are probably worried about your privacy in general. With the VPN, you can easily gain a lot of benefits in the long run. Other than that, in a nutshell, the application of a VPS highly plays a concrete role in ensuring that your web browser is more secure. In essence, you shall also be learning more about how to take advantage of its applications when you are attempting to gain access to sensitive information from your systems. As such, a VPN will come in handy not only when it comes to securing such privacy but ensuring that even the closest person to your office or home cannot gain access to the same data.

√ Update Your Passwords Often

As of now, you should be aware that it's vital to have unique employee passwords, unlike the common 123s that is appended to their dates of birth. Besides using the passwords that have features such as letters and numbers, in addition to uppercase letters, employees can be advised to often change their passwords and use business passwords in case there is a system that provides that option. In that case, you can work closely with the team to help in creating new passwords. But, that's not enough since you shall be required to incorporate the application of new passwords and change them every two months. Even with that in place, you shall still be required to create additional passwords that can be used by new entrants into the organization. For added security in the firm, you should consider training your workers to secure their passwords and network security with VPN and firewall. In fact, these are some of the most important details that you should share with your team in the office. Your business should also have its own computers in order to upgrade and enhance your security system and needs.

✓ Keep All Patches Updated

Because cyber-criminals are known for exploiting vulnerable operating systems, web browsers, as well as software applications, you need to secure your operating system and general networking system by using certain security measures. To be specific, you should be able to verify that your office computers are generally running their current versions using these programs:

- Adobe Acrobat, as well as Readers

- Oracle Java

- Microsoft Office Suite

- Internet Explorer

With that in mind, you need to keep a viable inventory in order to make sure that your devices are updated often. This should include mobile devices and network hardware. You should also make sure that Apple, as well as Windows laptops, have some automatic updating enabled in their systems. The inappropriate privileges granted to users also pose some threat to security measures imposed on various computer systems. With that in mind, it becomes important for employees to gain access to vital data regularly. This should be, by no means, overlooked. Over 4,000 firms have recently undergone some survey by the HP and the Ponemon Institute. The team leaders admitted that workers luckily had access to confidential information provided outside the main scope of job requirements. In a report finding by the same professionals, it was deduced that general business data, including documents and spreadsheets of the unstructured data, was mostly at risk when it comes to snooping. Customer data was also considered to be in a risky docket, given that it could be hacked by different people. The IT departments of these organizations were highly considered to be secure in different ways. As such, when a worker's job changes, it becomes crucial for the department to be notified of their departure so that the privileges to gain access to vital information can be modified in the long run.

✓ Using network security software

It is important that you are able to cover all the bases when it comes to network security. This is why it is important to have with you a wide variety of hardware and software tools. The firewall, for instance, is a vulnerable layer of protection, as you will need to fight the threats, both in front and behind the firewall. You will need to deploy some relevant tools to help you keep track of what is happening within the network including corporate products from some of the largest vendors, and some may be in the form of free, open-source securities that have been used by system administrators over the years. To have an efficient system, you must understand how easy or difficult it would be to penetrate the system. You may, therefore, have to engage in some form of ethical hacking to help you determine how efficient you are as a network.

The benefits of insisting on network security cannot be underestimated. As an enterprise existing in the digital world, it is important to deliver only the best to clients. Each company challenges itself to be the best, and this can only happen when the network is well-protected. Network security is a big part of the services offered by a company, as data breaches can usually lead to brand names becoming unpopular and businesses losing clients. It is, hence, important that network security shields the network from external threats, such as potential data breaches.

Conclusion

Thank you for reading the book *Computer Networking First Steps* to the very end. I am indeed glad that you made it far, and I hope against all hope that the book was informative and that it provided you with a platform on which you could learn the details of computer networking. With this information, I hope you can start on the journey toward the realization of your dreams, whatever they may be. I urge you to read extensively even after making it to the last page of this book because there is still so much that you can learn from other sources when expanding your horizon.

After reading this book, it is only logical that you will be better prepared to venture into networking at any capacity since the book offers you a boost in the knowledge you possess in this field. If you find that you still need help understanding some concepts, then it would be important that you continue reading and, possibly, consult with peers or professionals in the field.

The book is a source of a wealth of knowledge that is needed in navigating the everyday networks we come across or much more complex networks that you may need to interact with.

Once you have finished reading this book and understood the essentials of networking, you may find that you are better placed but still need refinement from other sources. You will, however, most certainly be prepared to approach networking at all levels.

If you found this book useful and resourceful, then please leave a review on Amazon; your efforts will be greatly appreciated.